# Z-Axis

# Z-Axis

*The Missing Link in Leadership*

Kevin Mannoia

*Foreword by Terry Taber*

WIPF & STOCK · Eugene, Oregon

Z-AXIS
The Missing Link in Leadership

Wipf & Stock
An Imprint of Wipf and Stock Publishers
199 W. 8th Ave., Suite 3
Eugene, OR 97401

www.wipfandstock.com

PAPERBACK ISBN: 979-8-3852-5367-8
HARDCOVER ISBN: 979-8-3852-5368-5
EBOOK ISBN: 979-8-3852-5369-2

VERSION NUMBER 09/30/25

# Contents

# Illustrations

# Foreword

WHEN MY FRIEND AND colleague, Kevin Mannoia, mentioned he was writing a book on leadership, two thoughts came to mind. First, what a challenging task, since books on leadership have appeared for many decades—so, what's new? But immediately I wanted to read what he was writing, since I have observed and learned from his leadership for more than a decade.

As I was reading his manuscript, the concepts on personal formation deeply resonated with me and my experiences as a leader. Early in my career, I was fortunate to be part of two organizations that invested in leadership development via formal and experiential training led by other leaders in the organization. Both organizations were focused on the personal aspects of leadership, which align with Mannoia's in-depth description of personal formation and the elements leading to the character of personhood for a leader.

In one of the two organizations, leadership development was called leadership discovery, and it was facilitated by internal leaders over a three-day offsite workshop. The word "discovery" was selected, since becoming a leader is a journey, not a destination. It is a discovery process about oneself as a person and that person, you, as a leader. As a result of being a participant and a "leader facilitator" of these leadership workshops, I was equipped with a strong foundation to lead the organization through a technology, market, and financial disruption. And, recently, I have been leading the transformation of the organization into a focused set of growing businesses. A key aspect in both examples was the non-anxious presence I was able to bring as a leader that allowed all of us to focus on what needed to be done rather than being tossed about by the chaos of change. What I learned and facilitated in the leadership workshops built confidence and certainty in me as a leader.

Mannoia's *Z-Axis: The Missing Link in Leadership* reviews the traditional dimensions of leadership, competence, and capacity while positioning character as a third leadership dimension. He suggests competence, capacity, and character need to be integrated, and in so doing you can begin to see the leader as WHOLE. For me, this integration of character with skills and potential is at the heart of discovery to become, and remain, an effective leader. Mannoia details characteristics of personal formation (character) for leadership and personal incentive and satisfaction for the individual pursuing such formation. He also addresses the "so what?" question, or "what difference does it make?"

I found this book to be a delightful and encouraging read. The worlds of business, education, countries, and many other organizations operate in a time where change happens often, and sometimes it happens rapidly. After reading this book, I was re-energized to mentor, develop, and prepare multi-dimensional leaders that bring competence, capacity, and character to their team, organization, or spheres of influence. Such leaders can and will make a difference. I hope you enjoy reading as much as I did.

Terry R. Taber, PhD
Senior VP, Advanced Materials & Chemicals
CTO, Vice-President, Eastman Kodak Company

August 2025

# Acknowledgements

*"THERE IS REALLY NOTHING new under the sun!"* The great King Solomon sought for deeper meaning and value in every conceivable corner of life and ultimately came to this conclusion. The best we can hope for is to discover what is already around us and to understand it in deeper, more nuanced, and effective ways.

What I discuss in this book is nothing new, but it may be completely different than anything you have ever read or considered in all of your study to become a corporate executive or HR specialist. In this book, I attempt to bring together two lines of thinking that have often remained separated but which, when integrated, show a powerfully impactful truth about working with people as a workforce and building systems of recruitment, evaluation, and development.

In conversations with a wonderful friend, Steven Bush, we have blended otherwise separate lines of thinking to offer you an entirely new level of influence in employee development. Steven is an entrepreneur with vast experience in the field of human resources, specifically at Target and Activision. Subsequently, he founded Kingdom One, a non-profit resource organization specializing in helping smaller organizations with excellence in HR and operational systems.

After reading one of my previous books, *The Integrity Factor*, Steven became excited with the impact that leadership formation could have on HR systems. Together with my interest in helping business and organizational leaders think differently about their workforce, we scribbled designs and ideas on the napkins at Klatch Coffee during our meetings.

In hopes of having new resources for you, as well as the Kingdom One clients, I have attempted to capture the spirit of this new pattern of thinking in this book. While serving as an introductory volume, I am convinced that in the hands of highly capable practitioners like you, these principles will be developed, implemented, and expanded to provide a profound "next level" of corporate/organizational management of people in businesses, non-profits, churches, and schools.

I am also indebted to some other great friends who took valuable time to read the manuscript early and give me honest feedback and input. Thank you to Dean Kato, Deborah Wilds, Terry Taber, David Goodnight, Kip Palmer, Frank Vizcarra—and my wife, Kathy!

With more resources in the works to help you with practical implementation, I commend this book to you in hopes that you will explore the possibilities—not only to bring profit and success to your company, but also to bring hopeful flourishing to your people. That is the best investment you can make and the most impactful legacy you can leave!

Kevin Mannoia
August 2025

# Chapter 1

# Panorama of Possibilities

IS THERE ANYTHING LEFT to write about leadership? It seems as if all that can be discovered has been. The challenge is to find new, creative, innovative, and captivating ways to explain what appears to have become a completed understanding of the concept of leadership. A wide variety of methods to enhance interest and gain attraction have emerged in both the non-profit and for-profit arenas. In many respects, we have decided that the idea of leadership is fixed; now we just have to be more creative in selling it to companies and organizations—whether through increased volume, mesmerizing illustrations, or memorable turns of phrase.

Leadership has been packaged and parsed into styles and theories and practices—all of which require training and learning certain activities to perfect. It is often seen as a science that must be mastered. When applied, leadership is reduced to behaviors that, if practiced with skill, will have a desired effect. The difficulty is that by doing this, we miss a very important element in leadership. Style and skill are the shell. Like a hermit crab, the occupant of the shell is much more organic and complex than the shell itself. That organic, complex part of leadership cannot be simply acquired in a seminar and then applied through behavioral training. Leadership

1

styles are like a coat that we put on. We want it to fit, but it cannot replace the essence of the person who wears it.

In this book, we want to explore the deeper foundations of leadership that give life and vibrancy to the various styles that leaders may take on. It's important to probe what I call "the bottom of the iceberg" and not merely settle for analyzing the top. This is where leadership finds its power, resilience, confidence, and perseverance.

## LIMITED VIEW

Whole systems of organizational structure have been built around a presumed understanding of leadership as a two-dimensional science that results in output and the possibility of increased capacity. Recruitment, deployment, assessment, and resourcing seem to focus exclusively on what a leader actually produces and the hope that with some help, they can actually produce more.

Contemporary human resources departments all share a common paradigm of the "9-Box Grid," which explains and guides this two-dimensional understanding. The 9-Box HR tool is a talent management framework used to evaluate and map employees based on their performance and potential. It consists of a 3 x 3 grid with two axes—X and Y. The X-axis represents performance (low, medium, high), and the Y-axis represents potential (also low, medium, high). By plotting individuals on this matrix, organizations can identify high-potential employees who are strong performers and may be ready for leadership roles. Supervisors can also identify those employees who may need development or reassignment. The 9-Box model is used in discussions around succession planning, but mostly it is helpful in leadership development and strategic decisions regarding talent distribution within the company because it provides a clear visual snapshot of the workforce.

Each of the nine boxes along the X and Y axes in the grid represent a combination of high, medium, or low levels of both attributes—performance and potential. The top-right box, labeled "High Potential/High Performance," is often called "Future

Leaders" or "Stars," indicating top talent ready for advancement. The top-left, "High Potential/Low Performance," might be termed "Emerging Potential" or "Inconsistent Performers," suggesting individuals who need development or engagement. The bottom-right, "Low Potential/High Performance," is often called "Solid Performers," indicating reliable contributors with less growth trajectory. The center boxes—such as "Moderate Potential/Moderate Performance"—reflect steady but less exceptional talent, while the bottom-left box, "Low Potential/Low Performance," may be labeled "Underperformers" who often require critical review for improvement or transition. These titles help HR and leadership teams make informed decisions on development, succession planning, and resource allocation.

Supervisors use the 9-box grid to visually plot employees based on the two key dimensions of performance and potential. Performance is typically measured by how well an employee meets or exceeds job expectations, often based on recent evaluations or KPIs. Potential reflects their ability to grow into more complex roles or leadership positions. Supervisors evaluate each employee on these dimensions and place them in one of nine boxes on the grid along the X- and Y-axis, ranging from low performance/low potential to high performance/high potential. This helps identify high-potential talent for development, those who are performing well in current roles, and those who may need coaching or role adjustments.

Clearly this brief description is incomplete in describing the technology and complexity of those functions, but it underscores the point that current views of leadership, and therefore leaders, are two-dimensional. In other words, they are simply identified by their outcomes and potential for improvement. Leadership assessment systems, HR evaluative practices, and even tests to help determine giftedness and ability all revolve around the two key elements of performance and potential for improvement.

With this limited and bounded concept, the natural tendency for anyone wanting to focus on leadership is to start with those two key elements and try to figure out how to make them better—more results and capacity for more. What emerges is an almost singular focus on skill acquisition. Teaching people how to do leadership is the only option. Raising skill levels is the only way to see better results and to grow as a leader—do more; do better; do smarter. The hope is that when these happen, production will be greater, promotions will happen, and your capacity for influence will expand. In this environment, skill is the currency by which leadership is grown, and training is the methodology.

## LIMITATIONS OF TWO DIMENSIONS

A two-dimensional pattern of leadership might be easily manageable, measurable, and described. But it seems to result in a concomitant underdeveloped understanding of the one who exercises that leadership. If we define leadership only in two dimensions—performance and potential—pretty soon leaders simply become the agents of those same two dimensions. In managing people, then, we will limit ourselves only to that two-dimensional vision and reduce the person, our employee, to merely competence and capacity.

Two things happen when that minimalistic process occurs.

1. Those charged with managing people will begin to see their employees merely as assets to manage toward the productivity of the company. Something fundamental occurs within the mind and heart of the supervisor/manager as their own worldview and perspective of other people in their sphere is reduced to the limitations of a flat, two-dimensional vision. Motivation for their employee devolves to assessing whether that person can perform or not. Recognition of the inherent human value is lost in favor of the mercenary part that employee plays in the greater corporate objective. The synergy of limitless human development gives way to functional contribution. Seeing leadership merely as two functions of competence and capacity causes us to see leaders as cogs in the wheels of success. Even if the supervisor has some interest and commitment to the human dimension of the employee

and seeks to improve that, it is frequently driven by the desire to increase performance and output for the good of the organization.

2. A second result of that minimalistic mindset is that those charged with managing people will compartmentalize their employees into two categories: their work life and their private life. Interest in the private life will only exist to the extent that it has an impact on the work—positive or negative. Everything at work will become separate from their personal development, and any connection will be incidental or viewed through the lens of work results. Although rather simplistic, this bifurcation shows up in many complex and nuanced ways. Limiting the view of employees in this way by managers misses significant opportunities for much larger influence and effect. Furthermore, it creates a paradigm and environment in which employees recognize that bifurcation. In order to fit in and please the company, they too begin to see themselves as private or professional and to live compartmentalized lives. Extreme segmentation of life can easily become the source of intrinsic tension, imbalance, and loss of meaning.

## WHAT IF?

What if there were a third dimension? What if the development of leaders by HR teams and managers was not limited to merely adding value on a two-dimensional framework? What if a third element were introduced that opened a panorama of possibilities and a limitless expanse of growth potential through value that is multiplied?

# Chapter 2

# Leadership Is More Than Function

## ESSENTIAL NATURE

EVERY TIME I ASK a group of people the question "what is leadership?," I get a variety of answers. Often, there are as many responses as there are people. Everyone seems to see leadership through a different lens. But in some fundamental way, we all recognize leadership when we see it whether we define it alike or not. Answers include things like vision-casting, management, decision-making, administration, defining reality, leading people in a particular direction, integrity, and so on. Furthermore, examples of obvious leaders are often used to demonstrate what cannot be defined. Churchill, King, Thatcher, Greenleaf, Kennedy, Gandhi, Reagan, Jesus, Palmer, Saint Paul, Mandela . . .

Leadership is usually easier to recognize than to define. There is an intangible element to those who we recognize as effective leaders. It's a certain element that we just sense but cannot describe. The results are clearly evident, and in many cases the process or actions are diverse. But some common, underlying element seems to be present like a golden strand that runs through it all.

In an effort to understand it and define it, students of leadership will dissect and analyze patterns of behavior, observe particular skills that are repeatable, and synthesize principles that emerge. The result is that we develop theories and the science of leadership which is largely skills-based and objectifiable. The whole goal is to understand so that we can teach and replicate good leadership. There's nothing wrong with that—unless it becomes the sum total of what we understand leadership to be. Reducing the complexity of leadership to a set of behaviors or skills eviscerates its full impact and nature. And it implies that leadership is merely a skill or activity to be learned and applied.

However, when each of us looks at those leaders we admire, we recognize that their lives, leadership, and impact cannot be reduced merely to a set of activities that are the result of skill. There is something intuitive and intrinsic about those leaders that transcends our analysis. After all the analysis of actions and skills is done, when we boil it down, leadership is simply influence. Nothing more. Everything beyond that is a study in method or effect.

The complicating factor is that influence is manifested in a variety of ways with many different results. It's seen differently in different contexts. In the military, perhaps it is seen as "taking the hill." In diplomacy, perhaps it's equated with bringing diverse people together. While it is clear that influence is at work, the result and outcome might be very different, and even how that influence is exercised is quite varied.

When people have an effect on others, that is leadership. That's influence—and leadership is simply influence. It really doesn't matter in what role or capacity that influence occurs. It could be influence with many or with few or with only one. Ideally the influence will be positive, but sometimes it is not. The hope is that we can recognize the influence we have on others and channel that through myriad abilities and actions to a positive and constructive outcome. And hopefully by perfecting specific skills, we can increase the effect of that influence. But at its core, leadership remains simply influence.

It's much like the role that salt plays in influencing food. To many it provides flavor; to others it preserves; and to still others it adds nutrition. Common to each is the fact that it influences the context where it is applied. While we might define, analyze, and describe the effect, the essential nature of salt transcends both its circumstances and its effect. Something inherent within salt provides what is essential to its application and the outcome that results. But we all recognize that salt is at work. For us to define salt merely in terms of its application minimizes it and limits its effect.

## KEEPING IT WHOLE

For us to reduce the idea of leadership to merely a set of skills that, when applied, yield certain results misses the essential nature of leadership as influence. When we do that, leadership is crippled and limited. Furthermore, it negates the nature of the primary agent of leadership, which is people. We miss out on the fullness of that intangible fountainhead from which it flows. Skill training and activities are important. They serve to focus and multiply the effect of leadership in specific situations. But they should not be understood or developed apart from the deeper essential element that makes leadership whole.

Because the principle agency of leadership is people, it helps to understand that people are not compartmentalized beings. We were created as whole, integrated, social beings. In that dynamic complexity, we discover the fountainhead of all leadership. It's like discovering the bottom of an iceberg that is unseen but which supports and gives expression to the top that people can see. That unseen part of the iceberg is what provides the intangible element to effective leadership that transcends skill or style. The bottom of the iceberg provides nature, stability, texture, and direction to the skills and styles that are visible.

It is impossible to separate the various parts of a person. We are holistic. We have passion and emotions; we have intellect and reason; we have willfulness and choices; and we also have physicality and behaviors, which are the expressions of the person.

8

Although our contemporary performance culture tends to focus developmental efforts on external behaviors, attempting to train one dimension of a person without the other is counter to our nature as holistic beings. And, it further compartmentalizes that person and reduces their value as well as the effectiveness of the work they do. Conversely, treating an employee as a whole being—recognizing their inherent nature and the importance that nature plays in their daily behavior—will bring fullness and flourishing.

Many famous leaders in history recognized that the only way to truly bring transformation to a person and to an organization is to harness all dimensions of how we were made—head, heart, and hand. One famous leader of the 18th century, who began a movement that has fueled one of the most impactful currents in history, built his entire life on the basis of this threefold framework: people are truly transformed when all dimensions are integrated.[1]

Further, the way people learn and grow is much broader than merely by training. For true and deep transformation to occur in employees, all aspects of their nature must be included and affected. Although one dimension of our nature may become the entry point for new learning, we learn best when all dimensions are integrated—our intellect, our passion, our social engagement, and our behavioral patterns. Simply telling someone to do something may not have nearly the same effect as engaging these various dimensions of how they are transformed. We may "teach" a new principle or task that makes sense intellectually. But until the other elements of our being are touched and included, true transformation has not occurred. Or, for example, when our passion is captured with a new idea and our intellect, social thinking, and behavior are fully integrated with that passion, then we become truly transformed and effective.

1. John Wesley, an 18th-century religious leader, structured his efforts on the many aspects of human life, not just the spiritual. Many of his writings were in the area of health and finance, but he principally addressed the spiritual conditions of his era and engaged with legislative, economic, and social concerns. He did so by appealing to the intellectual, emotional, and behavioral aspects of persons in a fully integrative process. As a result, scores of religious institutions and many denominations spawned from these principles to become one of the fastest-growing collection of organizations in history.

## TRAINING AND FORMATION ARE DIFFERENT

One of the reasons I introduce the concept of formation in the process of developing leaders is to underscore the difference between growing in skill development and personal flourishing. When we "train" a person, we simply teach them to "do" certain skills that, when applied, should have a desired result. This kind of training also helps us to ensure that everyone is doing the same thing.

Usually, when we train people we start with the outcome in mind. What is the ideal result we seek? And what are the particular skills that most efficiently achieve that result? Once we find that recipe, leadership development can easily devolve into skill training that may be reduced to behavioral modification. With the right incentives, we can equip people with skills. Then, with high levels of efficiency, they will produce what we want. The incentive may be money, promotion, recognition, control, or any of a number of other factors used to motivate people. The result may certainly be high performance and great results, but at what cost? And what does it say about the company or manager who begins with results and may only see employees as a means to an end?

Training is reinforced by the visible and reproducible functions of analysis, repetition, and modified behaviors. Much of the literature in leadership is built upon the premise that improving skills will cause better leadership. While this is true, it is a limited view.

Please don't think I am opposed to outcomes and results. Performance is a key element of the burden of leadership placed upon anyone who holds that stewardship role within a company or organization. Because it is a trust placed in the leader by the organization, and because we are stewards of that trust, it's very important to treat that trust with high respect and even reverence. Outcomes, results, profits, production, and competence are the expectations. And they all demonstrate respect, discipline, and gratitude for the role we are given.

However, remember the premise we began with: people are the principal agents of leadership; people are created with many dimensions in an integrated fashion; therefore, the essence of a person is the fountainhead of performance and gives substance to skills.

Accepting this means that in leadership the essence of a person is of equal or greater value to performance. From that source of personhood all activities will flow and be shaped. So, it is incumbent upon us to pay attention to the formation of the person to an equal or greater degree than we give to skill acquisition. The essence of a person gives meaning and life to the activities they engage in. Skills become an expression of who the person is. They are a reflection of the person themselves. Keeping these dimensions fully in view affords the possibility for leaders to influence in a holistic and integrated way. And it helps us to focus on the development of leaders in a way that is consistent with how they have been created.

Furthermore, and perhaps most importantly, the outcomes that result are not merely because we have provided the right incentive and skill training. Results become a synergistic effect of the essence of a person finding expression in what they do. Motivation for performance shifts from simply responding to incentives to becoming a holistic expression of oneself in an overflow of who they are. That is flourishing.

Of course, forming a person is not reducible to a simple science. Though we may be tempted to apply specific tasks to every person in our attempts to form them as people, that falls prey to the very thing we are attempting to mitigate. Holistic, integrative, and deeply formative practices may look different for each person since each is unique in personality, gifting, and context. But there are principles that help to shape leaders. A term coined in the last thirty years in my book *The Integrity Factor*, captures the essence of this holistic and integrated effort. Leadership Formation is a careful integration of developing leadership skills and forming the person as the agent of leadership.[2]

---

2. Leadership Formation is a term introduced and described in greater detail in my book *The Integrity Factor*, in which the principles of spiritual formation and leadership development are integrated on a journey of formation.

# Chapter 3

# Crisis or Limitation?

Is THERE REALLY A crisis in leadership? Everybody seems to talk about the dearth of leaders and leadership. In response, we have built leadership schools and programs, write more about it, teach skills, conduct studies, and beat the drum of leadership. But is it really as acute as it seems? After all, there are a lot of really smart and highly skilled people all around. Talent and passion don't seem to be waning from generation to generation. From the Greatest Generation to the builders and boomers, all the way through Generations X, Y, and Z, up to the current generation, it seems that people are highly capable. Although patterns and issues have changed, passion abounds, as does talent and gifting. So, is there really a crisis of leadership, or are we simply losing sight of a key ingredient? Is it possible that due to the natural cultural progression toward increased specialization and empirical results, we are losing sight of the unseen but potent element of forming leaders?

## LEADERSHIP DEVELOPMENT

Human nature tends to focus on what is observable and empirically measurable—things like skill, tactics, strategy, and theory. We are tangible creatures. Whatever we can see, touch, feel, and measure are the commodities we attempt to develop. Often, we relegate the unseen to the realm of the spiritual and dismiss it as irrelevant or unnecessary in the pursuit of outcomes. By studying behaviors and actions, we can actually determine which ones and under what circumstances they produce most. Then it's easy to analyze those behaviors by breaking them into specific skills and activities. From that, we may create our list of training manuals that teaches aspiring leaders to perform those tasks in order to achieve the results with high probability.

Leadership development, then, becomes a predictable process of training a person to willfully choose to do specific tasks. With practice, they can repeat skills that tend to produce the best results. Those skills may even be to focus on the employee: *If I walk the halls and drop in on my people, they will feel that I care and it will make them perform better.* There's nothing wrong with that as a means to increase skills and raise production. But, the underlying motivation is simply to produce. We could even say that the ulterior motive of "being nice to employees" is to manipulate them into greater production, and it leaves the soul of a person out of the equation. If there is no intrinsic motivation, that kind of development of skills can lead to a hollow form of influence that presumes a person is merely a tool to achieve outcomes.

In its extreme, practicing such a limited understanding of leadership can easily cause burnout, shallowness, and loyalty that is merely a function of external incentives—like relevance, prestige, and power.[1] These may turn into the objective of an aspiring leader. Allowing these kinds of objectives to become the goal of one's life will ultimately create a person that has little depth of understanding to the meaningful questions of life and their own flourishing. A man by the name of Henri Nouwen, a profound 20th-century spiritual leader, describes the trap these objectives can set for the person whose life is driven by their pursuit.[2]

1. An accomplished scholar and professor at Notre Dame, Harvard, and Yale, Henri Nouwen, in his book *In the Name of Jesus*, identified relevance, prestige, and power as the major temptations faced by leaders, causing existential distraction.

2. Nouwen recognized that in spite of his accomplishments, he was living

## PERSONAL FORMATION

It's at this point that the idea of personal formation becomes highly important. Because the nature of a person is less visible and harder to define with precision, it is difficult to apply the same idea of development to our own growth. While leadership development largely refers to skill acquisition, personal formation treats a person as a multi-faceted, complex, and often intangible essence—things like balance, emotional health, moral compass, intrinsic holism. That kind of formation does not lend itself to the same type of precise, repeatable skill training. The idea of formation is much more aligned with the nature of a person as a holistic and integrated being. When we see the value of personhood, it is more appropriate to engage in processes that will form the person.

Formation, though, is not as precise as skill development. There is a measure of ambiguity that is commensurate with the undefinable nature of a person. Formation also implies that there are many forms that may characterize a person. Every person will be formed in some way. So, for leaders, it's important to think carefully about their own formation and the big questions that will ultimately shape who they are.

- *"What kind of person do I wish to become?"*
- *"What is the form of my own life that will shape my leadership?"*
- *"What's the nature of my own life that motivates my actions in leadership?"*

Neglect of these important and formative questions leaves to chance a person's formation—likely to be influenced by the pressures around them. While skills may not be associated with personal formation, there are principles that characterize the journey of being formed. The power of a person's formation is great, since it is from the deep formation of a person that the activities and skills are shaped.

---

in a very dark place, which awakened him to understand that the term "burnout" was a "convenient psychological translation for his own spiritual death." Henri Nouwen, *In the Name of Jesus*, 15–16 (New York: Crossroad, 1989).

Two people may utilize the exact same skill in a leadership situation, but the result could be very different. The application of the particular skill is not enough. The nature or form of the person exercising that skill acts like a carrier wave, providing context, spirit, attitude, and disposition to the act itself. Of course, this raises the question as to whether it is really the skill activity itself that is effective or the nature of the person that determines success. Some of the most effective leaders may not have been highly competent in their leadership technique. But that intangible, undefined inner formation has multiplied the effect of their competence to make them highly effective.

In fact, effectiveness in leadership involves both of these dimensions—precision in the competent use of skills and depth of integration in the formation of their character and personhood. Competence without character leads to arrogance. People who are confronted with arrogant leaders will likely not respond well, no matter how proven the skill activity is. Conversely, character without competence winds up in irrelevance. A leader with sound character may be well liked and even respected, but if they are unable to skillfully lead, not only will the results cause failure, but people will grow weary of lack of performance.

In truth, both leadership development and personal formation are the important elements to effectiveness in raising new leaders into influence as well as in evaluation of those leaders already deployed. Hence our focus on Leadership Formation. Later, we will explore the integration of these two features in-depth through illustrative means.

## LEADERSHIP THEORIES

To put this new concept of Leadership Formation into greater clarity, let us take a brief look at the theories that have given rise to contemporary patterns of development and assessment.

Today, we generally use two axes (plural for *axis*, not a wood-chopping tool) for assessment and training. The X-axis deals with the observable patterns of behavior and skill acquisition that focus on outcomes and results—competence or performance. What are the actual results a person is achieving? Is their performance visible and moving in a positive direction? By these results we measure success—or lack thereof. Salary, recognition, and promotions are often tied directly to the X-axis of results.

The Y-axis treats the question of capacity or potential. Does this person have what it takes to move up? Do they have a future? Could they take on more responsibility? Although somewhat intangible, we have grown rather proficient in observing people and predicting their future trajectory. Mostly, it is tied to the axiom that "the best predictor of a person's future is their past performance." With a little extrapolation and vision, a person's potential can be described to a relatively significant degree of accuracy. These are the people who find themselves fast-tracked, or put into the executive program, or sent for more education—all as an investment in the future.

Generally, these two aspects of contemporary metrics derive from basic leadership theories that carry similar names. Particularly, Theory X leadership, which puts the principal focus on the task and its outcome. Measurable results in observable products or outcomes are the centerpiece to a Theory X management theory. Of course, there are important ramifications that come along with that premise. For example, if the task is the top priority, then people are merely a means to an end. Furthermore, the theory implies that people are inherently unmotivated and need external stimuli to cause performance to improve so that the task is more greatly achieved. They don't need to understand the "why" and merely need the proper motivation that will get them to perform.

Theory Y makes people the primary focus. Because people are the actual workers, they are the de facto capacity for outcomes; hence, they are the central focus. Theory Y also has implications as a management style. It presumes that people are self-motivated and will regulate themselves. While it places a higher value on the importance of the person, it still is concerned with outcomes insofar as well-cared-for people will produce better results. Further, it invests in the development of people largely by external means, like work environment, benefits, personal interest, and so forth. If we give our people good benefits and a good workplace, they will perform. But there is still a missing piece that remains unaddressed. We will take a closer look at that a bit more later.

Similarly, Blake & Mouton's "People/Task" grid framed management on a continuum anchored in each extreme by the two dimensions of focus—people and task. But again, even though for the first time in corporate organizational theory efforts were made to consider the worker as a person, it was largely as a means to an end.

X and Y are not new to corporate HR and leadership discussions. Deriving from these historic theories, modern derivations of these axes have come to be the basis of many human resource patterns and structures for hiring, assessment, and development. To a significant degree, HR practices and patterns today hinge upon these two major themes:

1. Competence—task, performance, results.

2. Capacity—potential, future results, ability to rise.

With all of the time, energy, and resources focused on the improvement of these two dimensions, often it seems that something is missing. From small examples in departments of small organizations to highly public, high-profile cases like a global financial crisis or a national mortgage meltdown, it seems that there is a missing link. Experience and observation create a deep curiosity and desire for something more. What if there were a third dimension?

But first, let's look more deeply at the two axes we've come to depend on.

# Chapter 4

# X-Axis

*Competence in Performance of Skills*

## TWO THEORIES

SO, LET'S TAKE A closer look at the two historic axes that have characterized the development of employees and especially leaders for many decades. First, the X-axis. During the 20<sup>th</sup> century, many studies of employee workforces, as well as the rising field of psychology and especially organizational psychology, provided innovations that altered the workplace. Douglas McGregor was a particularly important referent in the mid-20<sup>th</sup> century who introduced two distinct theories of motivation and management. Prior to this, getting the job done and producing results was paramount and the singular measure of success. Built on studies like the famous Hawthorne Studies between 1924 and 1932 in Chicago, things began to change as research showed that improvement in performance could be influenced by paying attention to the people—even if only increasing or decreasing the lighting levels, as was the case at the Hawthorne Electric Company. Yet, the whole object, even to those discoveries, was to increase performance.

While it may seem strange to appeal to research and theories that are a century old, it's quite interesting to note that the foundations articulated from that research remain central to the ongoing thinking around leadership and assessment today. Certainly, there are myriad resources that have refined our thinking, yet when we trace the roots of each one, they find a connection—either direct or indirect—to these historic conclusions. And most importantly, the very nomenclature used in hiring, evaluating, developing, and guiding people in businesses today is connected.

McGregor formulated two views of people especially related to their motivation and effectiveness—Theory X and Theory Y. These had important implications in the workplace and contributed to long-standing patterns of how organizations develop and measure work and how they evaluate employees.

## A CLOSER LOOK AT X

Basically, what he termed "Theory X" starts with the premise that people are fundamentally lazy and need an external motivation to keep productive. They also need specific direction in training to maximize output. Money or fear are the default motivations for that external motivation used by organizations based upon that assumption. The goal was to increase production. To do that individual employee performance was crucial. Pressure, fear, and financial incentive proved to be effective tools to motivate individuals to perform—at least in the short term. The concomitant measure in a Theory X management environment is that performance is the driving force behind success. Usually performance was easily measured since actual products were a tangible way to determine productivity.

Performance, then, was the objective of management as measured by outcomes and results. That was the basis of Theory X management. It is interesting then, that modern systems of human resources use the X-axis as a means to define performance. The basic assumption about Theory X management was that people are merely the instrument through which performance was achieved. Even today it is easy to fall prey to the idea that the employee is an instrument that needs to be "trained" to perform so that the outcomes of the organization are better. With this emphasis, employee recruitment, evaluation, development and discipline begin with the assumption that performance is the measure of one's value.

In the modern workplace, performance is often the defining lens through which we categorize employees as "good" or "bad." In many organizational settings, the concept of a "high performer" becomes the shorthand for who gets promoted, who receives development opportunities, and who is deemed indispensable. And in the recruitment of people, performance becomes the litmus test above other factors to determine the value of acquiring a particular person. As you can imagine, this simplistic binary thinking doesn't do justice to the full complexity of human contribution within an organization. Nor is it consistent with the nature of how people are created, which we've discussed in previous chapters. One of the most significant pitfalls of a simple binary approach to employee effectiveness is the narrow and sometimes misleading tools we have inherited—particularly the forced distribution systems and outdated performance appraisal frameworks. Let's look more closely.

## FORCED DISTRIBUTION

In many companies, forced distribution is mandatory. This method, often referred to as "rank and yank," requires that employee performance ratings conform to a predefined distribution —typically resembling a bell curve, or a statistical standard distribution. For example, perhaps the management regime determines that only 5 percent of employees can receive an "Outstanding" rating, while the majority (around 70 percent) must be categorized as "Meets Expectations" and a bottom percentage (10–15 percent) labeled as "Underperforming." The top group are identified as "outstanding" because of high performance in producing the particular outcomes that are determined to be valuable by the managers. The 70 percent that "meet expectations" are the majority that center around the mean—usually one standard distribution above and below the mean. The bottom group, who are "underperformers," become the target for intervention and out-counseling.

This approach, while efficient from a statistical standpoint, introduces real human costs. One example in the past of forced distribution was at General Electric. Managers were required to fire the bottom 10 percent of performers annually. This created a hyper-competitive atmosphere where people began to protect their ratings instead of collaborating. In the short-term this practice drove performance. But, it also led to fear-based leadership and long-term cultural shifts that created larger challenges for the organization.

Do you remember in school when the teacher made it clear that she or he "graded on the curve?" Simply put, it meant that everyone's grade was relative to each other. Rank was determined by the order each person achieved in performance. If everyone did poorly, the highest grade among the entire group was the A. On the other hand, if one person achieved at a very high level, thereby setting the standard for the top grade, the rest were required to perform well in order to get as close as possible to that good grade. So, usually, if your experience is the same as mine, students never liked that one person in the class that didn't care about how the others performed—they just always scored high. They skewed the curve upward, and the rest were scored relative to that. The students who were most worried were the ones who couldn't achieve at that level.

The intent behind forced distribution is to maintain high standards of production and reward excellence. However, its application usually creates low morale in employees and teams, competitiveness that undermines synergy and discourages initiative and innovation. It can even encourage unethical behavior by causing internal stress on people who choose to override their moral compass in order to achieve higher performance while undermining coworkers.

Another effect of a heavy emphasis on performance is that standards can easily change. They tend to evolve with organizational strategy and culture that is prescribed by management to chase the "bogey" of results. A performance target that may have once defined outstanding performance may no longer be so in an environment where expectations consistently rise or even simply change. Likewise, the "ideal employee" profile shifts from one standard of expected performance to another. Of course, this is not to decry the effort of leaders to continually call their teams to improve, but when it is simply based upon a rise in expectation merely for performance's sake, the role of the employee is relegated to a functional tool of achievement.

## THE EFFECT ON MANAGEMENT MINDSET

A secondary but equally important effect of a single-minded focus on performance occurs within the thinking of the leaders. When performance, or competence in producing output, is the focus of managers, the motivation in them to look beyond results wanes. There is little need to consider other factors, and the awareness of the real lives of the people is easily overlooked. The X-axis, when used singularly or predominantly creates management leaders and a system that defaults to transactional thinking, where the measure used is a simple assessment of performance.

This is not to say that performance should not be a significant factor in every organizational system. Clearly without performance, every organization—corporation, business, school, or church—will fail to fulfill its purpose and mission. The very intent of organizations is to fulfill some intent for which it was created. Educating young people, producing some product, making some difference, or meeting the needs of people spiritually. All of them are appropriate hoped-for outcomes of institutions. These outcomes can be measured and are achieved by competence in the performance of duties and functions associated with the nature of the organization. Performance is absolutely essential to the very purpose of organizations, never to be overlooked.

The point here is to clearly explain the X-axis, with its focus on performance, through competence of functional skills by people who are trained in those skills and properly deployed. But more importantly, to demonstrate the potential pitfalls of an over-emphasis on a culture and organizational system that emphasizes performance so much that it does not consider other equally important factors yet to be discussed. In the X-axis culture, the need for excellent performance and outcomes drives the need for competency in function. So, most employee development plans and leadership training programs will focus on competence in order to improve performance. While necessary, it overlooks the fullness of how people have been created and reduces the employee to mere skills that are acquired through proficient training.

When assessing a particular person on the X-axis of competence and performance in the 9-Box grid, someone who is in the High-Performance category is valuable. A moderate performer is understood to have under-utilized talent, and a low performer is a performance risk. These are important things to consider, certainly. But not to the exclusion of other equally significant dimensions that consider the wholeness of a person and the complexity of organizational culture and effectiveness.

# Chapter 5

# Y-Axis

*Capacity for Potential Influence*

## A CLOSER LOOK AT Y

THE X-AXIS ON THE 9-Box grid represents the current performance of an individual staff member or employee. It's based upon results and how well they master the skills of their current role. It is fairly easy to measure by use of performance reviews and whether key performance indicators have been met. By contrast, the Y-axis is much more nuanced in focusing on leadership capabilities. It represents future potential. Specifically, how well a person may grow into the higher levels of leadership roles and their capacity to assume more complex responsibilities.

Quickly after discovering the importance of performance as a key measure of success, the same 20th-century studies previously mentioned showed that people were an important variable. The Hawthorne researchers from Harvard Business School, led by Elton Mayo, concluded that it wasn't more lighting or less lighting that improved performance, but it was the fact that the people were actually being observed and noticed. They performed better when the lighting was increased as well as when it was decreased. This phenomenon is known as the Hawthorne Effect—people modify their behavior when they know they are noticed. People are important.

McGregor's second theory seemed to build upon that assumption. If Theory X is all about performance, Theory Y is about people—and the potential they represent in being able to adjust, grow, and adapt. Theory Y begins with the premise that people are intrinsically motivated, and the job can be rewarding and satisfying to them. With self-direction and internal confidence, they can move toward personal and corporate achievement. People can learn to take on responsibility, and they have capacities that can be tapped into for greater fulfillment. In short, people possess high potential for innovation, adaptability, and resourcefulness to solve and fulfill organizational challenges. Again, the connection with modern 9-Box axes is not coincidental where the Y-axis represents potential in someone's future. Potential in a person informs questions of succession, promotion, and possible adaptability, which drive recruitment, development, and evaluation systems.

To get a more complete understanding of the typical 9-Box Grid, if it is new to you, here is what it looks like. In some cases, the specific terms that describe each quadrant might be somewhat different, but the framework and the principles remain the same across all applications.

| Low Performer/<br>High Potential | Moderate Performer/<br>High Potential | High Performer/<br>High Potential |
|---|---|---|
| ➢ Possibly mismatch of role & capability<br>➢ Growth potential with resources | ➢ Emerging leader with development<br>➢ Ready for stretch assignments | ➢ Future leader candidate<br>➢ Invest in retention and involve in considerations for succession |
| DEVELOP | DEVELOP/STRETCH | STRETCH |
| **Low Performer/<br>Moderate Potential** | **Moderate Performer/<br>Moderate Potential** | **High Performer/<br>Moderate Potential** |
| ➢ Shows glimpses of promise<br>➢ Needs coaching and development | ➢ Steady contributor with medium growth potential<br>➢ Candidate for lateral moves | ➢ Strong performer with growth possibility<br>➢ Consider enhanced responsibilities |
| OBSERVE | DEVELOP | DEVELOP/STRETCH |
| **Low Performer/<br>Low Potential** | **Moderate Performer/<br>Low Potential** | **High Performer/<br>Low Potential** |
| ➢ Limited impact<br>➢ May require reassignment or exit strategy | ➢ Reliable in current role<br>➢ May lack capability or drive for mobility upward | ➢ Expert in current role<br>➢ Limited future advancement but valuable contributor |
| OBSERVE / EXIT | OBSERVE | DEVELOP |

POTENTIAL — Y Axis

X Axis -- PERFORMANCE ➡

The Y-axis on the 9-Box tool is particularly intended to help map the ability of people to take on more responsibility and complex leadership. Based upon past trajectory in a person's leadership and work, it is used to determine the chances of a person moving through advancement. It helps the organizational systems and leaders to determine who to accelerate through developmental systems of promotion to reach their full potential.

Assessment around the Y-axis generally is based on evidence of key traits most commonly associated with higher levels of responsibility. The driving question is whether a person is likely to succeed in higher leadership roles in the future. By observing the past patterns of behavior, insightful assessment can predict with significant accuracy the probability of future effectiveness. These are often the ones who are placed in executive tracks or leadership "farm-systems" with a development plan. A person identified in the upper rows of the 9-box grid are usually identified as "high potential" (HiPo) employees. The Y-axis keeps supervisors asking the question, *"Does this person have the capacity and intrinsic motivation to assume larger challenges and responsibilities in the future?"*

## DEVELOPMENT PLANS AND FARM SYSTEMS

The use of development plans is the primary way to encourage people to grow. They serve as an anchor point between the X- and Y-axes. Once assessed, a personal development plan is tailor-made to help move a person to next levels in the areas most needed. If someone has high potential but is weak in performance, the plan will focus on remediating those performance skills as a way to prepare a person for future leadership at higher levels. For the one who is strong in performance but whose potential is unclear, a development plan may focus on stretching them, especially in the more nuanced elements of leadership that are less tangible and trait-oriented.

Development plans are particularly useful in Y-axis features like the development of future talent, succession planning, and in nurturing rising leaders for the future. Often progress on a development plan will determine whether someone is placed into an executive track or a leadership farm system that will eventually serve the highest leadership needs of the organization. They help by pinpointing areas where someone needs to grow so they can contribute to the future. They always are aligned with the organizational needs and allow supervisors or HR professionals to monitor growth in a person's capacity to fulfill their potential. As a side benefit, they also are used to engage and to retain the best talent. High Potential (HiPo) leaders are often the most sought after and are less motivated by salary than they are by a future pathway of growth.

Farm systems are extremely important features of encouraging a focus on the Y-axis. Much like the minor league baseball teams, a farm system serves to provide intentional training and development for those identified as future leaders. A strong system helps to mitigate negative impact when a vacancy occurs. Someone can easily be "brought up" from the farm team to fill the role.

Because of the nuanced nature of Y-axis development, a farm system is not as simple as merely skill-training. In Ron Heifetz terms, the technical leadership ability requires training, while adaptive leadership necessitates more development through circumstantial exposure to nurture key traits.[1]

Because of that, farm systems involve more features that develop specific competencies in a person thereby helping them in the future to expand organizational capacity for impact performance or output. These farm systems will provide for a rotation of assignments to test and develop intrinsic traits needed. Mentoring and coaching are an important feature wherein senior leaders are able to transfer knowledge and wisdom that is highly situational. HiPos may also be provided opportunities for further education to nurture both ability and loyalty. And of course stretch projects provide more visible situations to observe and test the progress of a potential leader in the evolution of key traits for future leadership.

The Y-axis gives an organization the ability to show commitment to its own future, which in turn breeds confidence and stability over the long-term. Failure to develop people can become a sure indicator of a limited future and be a costly gap to fill when vacancies occur and external hires are the only option. I've often heard it said, and I share this idea, that "the best leaders are home-grown." My ability as a senior leader to turn to one of my farm systems when I needed to was both liberating and highly fulfilling. And it provided the confidence that the internal DNA of the organization would still be in good hands and not threatened.

While the X-axis keeps things going today, the Y-axis ensures a bright future. Most importantly it inculcates the organizational identity and DNA into the future leaders in more than simply words or a half-day onboarding orientation. The priority on developing the potential leaders within an organization secures the corporate culture, which if ignored will become the silent killer.

---

1. Ronald Heifetz is the founder of the Center for Public Leadership at Harvard Kennedy School. He co-developed the adaptive leadership framework with Sinder and Linsky, distinguishing the challenges each poses to effective influence.

Many organizations use a Theory X environment today. That will result in tight controls, high supervision, and detailed skill training. It produces a reluctance to change and relatively low innovation, since the focus is on performance output. Likewise, many organizations utilize Theory Y in their workplace. That tends to result in decentralization, collaboration, and participative decision-making. Most importantly it encourages personal development and innovation, as well as nurturing the development of the person.

If we overlay Maslow's hierarchy of needs, which identifies the range of human needs, we could say that Theory X addresses the lower levels of human need like survival, physical need, and security. In Theory Y the higher levels are being addressed, like social needs, esteem, and ultimately self-actualization.

Looking back to previous chapters, a careful balance of these two axes are important features in the nature of how humans were created. We have a need to work, to produce, and to see results. But that proceeds from an inherent nature that aspires, grows, develops, integrates, and flourishes. While neither of these two axes is sufficient in themselves, both combined are also incomplete in capturing the fullness of people who are created with a fullness and wholeness that transcends either dimension. A third axis is necessary to capture our true nature and unleash our fullest potential for influence, transformation, and flourishing.

# Chapter 6

# Z-Axis

*Making It Whole*

## HIERARCHY OF NEEDS

THROUGH THE WORK OF Abraham Maslow and his hierarchy of human needs,[1] the view of people and what motivates them has expanded substantially. Rather than simply viewing a person as a repository of information that can be leveraged into job success or even applied as influence, the birth of organizational psychology began to expand our understanding that people are whole and are motivated by various needs. Maslow's hierarchy helps us to understand the innate needs people have, especially in their formative years. It begins with the most basic level of physiological needs for survival, then safety and security, love and belonging, esteem and recognition, and finally the highest need in this paradigm—the need for self-actualization.

Since that time, some of us have realized that even the concept of self-actualization has a limitation that is imposed by the very nature of our human finitude. In reality, we have been created as beings with a capacity to live in dimensions beyond our own

1. In 1943, American psychologist Abraham Maslow proposed five goals, or needs, that motivate human behavior. First introduced in the journal *Psychological Review*, typically they are depicted in a pyramid diagram.

physical limitations. That metaphysical level possesses some of the highest motivation for people to grow and be formed. While "self"-actualization is limited to the potential of a person, when the spiritual element of the nature that is imprinted upon us is considered, a much fuller actualization is truly a possibility. Since that nature has been placed within us by an infinite Creator, our potential for formation is likewise limitless. This is tied to an understanding of a Divine Other who created humans to begin with and in whom a person can find complete fulfillment, identity, and unlimited formation.

## INTRODUCING Z—ADDING THE MISSING LINK

To some extent developing the person is not new, but emphasizing personal formation as a third element in dialogue with the other two is. So, let's add a third axis to the existing two; and we call it "Z-axis." This should not be mistaken for Maslow's Theory $Z^2$ or William Ouchi's so-called "Japanese Management" style.[3] Nor is this to be confused with the Contingency or Situational leadership styles that emerged from those management theories. We speak of a third dimension of viewing leadership that adds to the X-axis (Competence) and Y-axis (Capacity). We now add Z-axis—Character.

It doesn't take much to realize that adding a third dimension to a pattern that is well-worn and established introduces significant implications and features. Beginning by seeing the leader as WHOLE results in an integration of all three dimensions from the start rather than simply connecting competence and capacity as a means to achieve the single purpose of success in performance— present and future.

The permutations of adding a third dimension to a standard assessment grid is multiplied, and complexity is increased

2. Maslow also suggested a "Theory Z" of management in an article he published in the *Journal of Transpersonal Psychology* in 1969.

3. In 1981, William Ouchi introduced a theory of management, responding to the Asian economic boom.

dramatically. The possibility of fully engaging the wholeness of an employee in their own flourishing is remarkable. The typical two-dimensional 9-box grid now becomes a three-dimensional cone, adding depth and dimension to the otherwise flat pattern of thinking for assessment and development.

> *Adding the Z-Axis to the traditional 9-Box multiplies the dimensions of possibilities for leaders to grow and flourish. For the organization that recognizes this potential, stewarding the formation of their people will become their greatest responsibility and reward.*

Think about evaluating an employee based upon the two traditional axes of performance and capacity. Now, can you imagine adding the Z-axis of character or personhood to that? Our ability to understand, evaluate, and develop our people becomes far more textured and potent. HR and leadership efforts can move beyond developmental evaluation and remediation into holistic formation. Tapping into the inherent identity of a person, together with their inner sense of being and calling, adds greater ability to lift and empower people to become their best selves.

Adding this dimension to the two other axes—X and Y—provides people with a whole new dimension. It gives the hope of truly flourishing as people and employees. Equally important, it provides employers, corporations, and HR departments with the reality that before us lies the possibility of tapping into the innate need of every person to find their fullest self—their intended fulfillment and growth toward the ideal of what they were created to become.

Opening ourselves to this reality of the human person as the agent of influence moves us beyond leadership as merely performance and outcomes. And it makes real the fountainhead of influence as being far more than merely success or incentive. True motivation comes from a deep well of fulfillment and an inner impetus to flourish as we were intended. In other words, to become all that we were meant to become in holistic, integrated completeness.

## A CLOSER LOOK AT Z

Every person will deal with the most profound emotions and circumstances possible. Rejection, fear, success, praise, relevance, power, recognition. If left with only the competence to perform well (X) in the face of any of these, or if only drawing upon the hope of our own capacity to rise above them (Y), people will wind up treating any of these as just another "work situation" to deal with. When we anchor ourselves in a deep and well-formed sense of identity, personhood, and character (Z), suddenly it's as if an intrinsic balance from the inside-out holds us stable in the face of the most extreme circumstances. Not dependent upon ability to "manage the situation," this axis of personhood becomes like the bottom of the iceberg that holds a person stable in the middle of storms. While the circumstances will not automatically disappear, a well-formed person sees those for what they are—external situations moderated by a sound character, freeing them to use their skills to lead through the situation rather than merely managing it.

So far, I have hinted at an illustrative depiction of this third dimension in working with people in Leadership Formation. Let me explain it visually to help us capture its importance. Then we can see it in relation to the two-dimensional pattern of current practice.

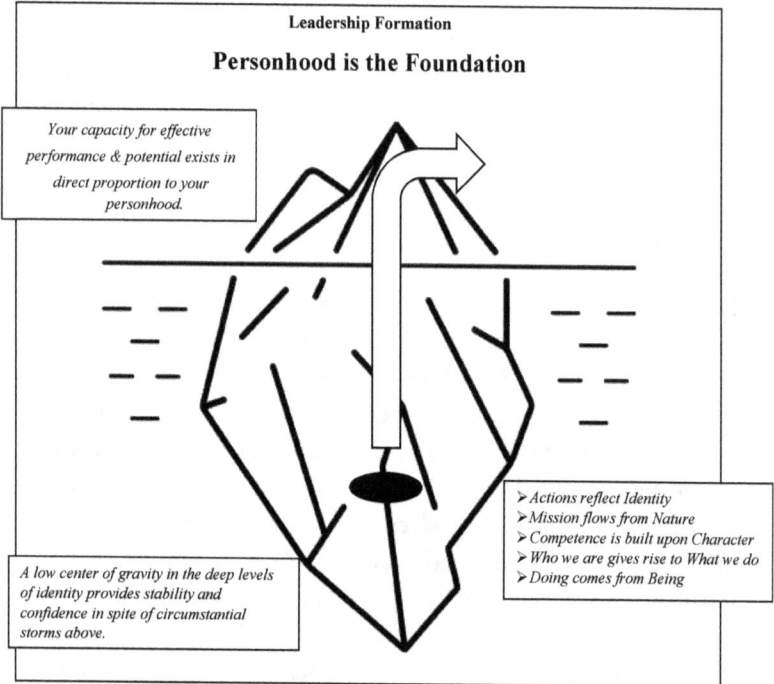

**Leadership Formation**

## Personhood is the Foundation

*Your capacity for effective performance & potential exists in direct proportion to your personhood.*

> Actions reflect Identity
> Mission flows from Nature
> Competence is built upon Character
> Who we are gives rise to What we do
> Doing comes from Being

*A low center of gravity in the deep levels of identity provides stability and confidence in spite of circumstantial storms above.*

Taken from the more comprehensive explanation of
the Iceberg in my book *The Integrity Factor.*

Identity gives rise to behavior. Who we are will always have an effect on what we do. Those are two dimensions of leadership that are inseparable. They are like two sides of the same coin. Better yet, it is like an iceberg. One tenth of the mass of an iceberg is found above the waterline. Nine tenths, then, lies beneath the waterline, where no one can see it. The top of the iceberg is in the visible realm; the bottom is unseen. There is one iceberg but two dimensions.

The top of the iceberg represents the leadership activities that we perform and which others may see and evaluate—vision-casting, management, budgets, decision-making, strategic planning, counseling, directing. The bottom of the iceberg represents the identity of the leader. It is much less measurable and often goes unseen by others. It definitely exists and is real. It is not invisible, just unseen. The bottom of the iceberg deals with the question "who am I?," while the top of the iceberg deals with "what am I here to do?" The top speaks to activity, performance, achievement, and competence. The bottom deals with the person's nature, formation, personhood, and character. Both are essential elements for a leader. But you can quickly see that one cannot exist without the other. The top is doing and the bottom is being. The top of the iceberg is only able to keep balance and stability to the extent that the bottom is well formed and deep.

A leadership style is merely the description of activities in the top of the iceberg and their effect on the surrounding context. It describes "how" a particular person engages and influences the surrounding context. Naturally, then, success in this realm is defined and measured in terms of results that come in tangible, visible, measurable outcomes. The pursuit of good leadership is merely the mastery of skills and activities that are applied with increasing competence in response to particular needs or situations. It is very circumstantial and quite tied to task success. If we think about leadership only as a style, we are assuming that outcomes or results are the priority and primary reference point for leadership. Effective leadership is reduced to simply being the mastery of prescribed skills rather than an intrinsic quality that is formed. The ability of leadership to be adaptive and respond to changing contexts becomes limited to the repertoire of skills in a particular leader. The capacity of the leader to discern the critical circumstances around them is reduced to merely observing the effect of a selected leadership behavior or style in the top of the iceberg.

In reality, wholeness and long-term effectiveness come from a much more integrated place. There's a whole other dimension that comes into play when we really engage with the fullness of Leadership Formation and true effectiveness. Effective leadership is formed in the synergy of building integrity between who we are and what we do, between the bottom and the top of the iceberg. To relegate leadership only to the category of a successful style limits it to the top of the iceberg, which is only a fraction of who the leader really is. Furthermore, seeing it only through the lens of a superficial style of behavior makes it entirely dependent upon the results of "doing" leadership.

Leadership Formation begins with the condition of the leader, and its priority is the formation of identity, nature, character—the bottom of the iceberg. That will organically and naturally give rise to activity that is consistent with its nature because that is how we were made. The bottom of the iceberg always provides a foundation and nature out of which activities in the top of the iceberg are performed.

This is not to say that "training the hand" with skills that are well-honed and useful in the top of the iceberg arena of performance is not important. It is to say, however, that proceeding from a well-formed bottom that is stable, deep, and whole will make competence in performance of even greater influence. And that influence will transcend the particular task or performance indicator and overflow into organizational culture as well as into the lives of those who are influenced. You see, we cannot separate who we are from what we do. They are inextricably intertwined.

## CENTER OF GRAVITY

I have often told young MBA students preparing to enter new levels of leadership that you don't manage complex and challenging circumstances simply with better skills. You start from a low center of gravity.

Every one of us in leadership has experienced times when it feels like we are trying to keep a lot of spinning plates going at once. More are added, and we try harder to manage them. Finally, one more comes and our competence is at its limit . . . they all come crashing down. Perhaps it takes the form of burnout, depression, resignation, or even cataclysmic failure in our role; family and marriage unravel; addictions take over as a way to anesthetize or distract. There are innumerable ways such a crisis can manifest. Usually those traumatic experiences are not simply the result of limitations of competence but of the growing realization that our growth capacity is strained. In response we may simply grit the teeth and try harder to manage our insecurity, fear, anxiety, or frustration. Managing the circumstances is not the path to balance or confidence.

Keeping a low center of gravity means that we understand the deep well from which our work and effort proceeds. We realize that our competence is informed, shaped, and sustained by our character. When the bottom of the iceberg is well formed, deep, and truly represents the major part of who we are, then the stresses of our circumstances become challenging but not catastrophic. We may be strained but not broken. Our identity is not defined by what we do or how well we do it. So, I would tell those same MBA students that the key to managing complex, challenging circumstances is to "center down." To be reassured in the low center of gravity that is deep below the water line—the nature of who you are as a person. Allowing that to be your center will bring balance to what you do.

A low center of gravity is not something that happens by chance. It is intentional. And it requires a willful choice on your part to develop, deepen, and invest in your own character, which in turn becomes your anchor and stabilizing center. Neglect can result in an ill-formed iceberg that can capsize easily.

Imagine where the center of gravity is on a well-formed iceberg. I am told by folks in geometry that usually the center of gravity is about one-third up from the bottom. Picture the iceberg, then. The one-tenth that you see above the waterline is entirely supported and stabilized by the 90 percent below. The center of gravity is in the bottom. Imagine a violent storm arising on the ocean. High waves batter the iceberg, lightning, winds, sleet—a furious storm. The top is completely exposed and suffers the effects of that storm. But a few hundred feet below the surface, where the center of gravity is, conditions are calm, peaceful, and quiet. That is the stabilizing core of the iceberg. It holds the entire berg steadfast in the face of the storm. The top may be bruised and battered, but the bottom holds it stable and secure through it all.

You see, every leader will find themselves in the middle of storms raging all about in their career. Circumstances beyond their control may create "the perfect storm." If they only depend upon their skills to maintain personal equilibrium and balance, they may fail. With a low center of gravity, they can withstand the assault of circumstances outside their control. They may be battered a bit in their position, function, even reputation and performance. But down deep, where the core of their identity is forged and formed, there is peace, quiet, and inner confidence that can hold them stable in the face of the storm.

Take another step and envision the many people around who are watching the iceberg. The part they see is only a fraction. But if, for a variety of reasons, they choose to attack, criticize, or "shoot" at the iceberg, they will only be able to target the top—it's all they can see. Whether out of envy, competition, politics, or just plain dislike, critics may target you as a leader. They may insult, attack, undermine, or oppose. But the only part of you they see is the top of the iceberg—your activities, your performance. While they may hope to do serious damage to you as a person, they can only attack what they see.

That kind of opposition can be crippling and personally debilitating to someone whose sense of identity is tied to their performance. Often it causes people to react viciously or irresponsibly in retaliation. It may result in harsh bitterness, angry outbursts, and even moral failures. But for the person with a well-formed iceberg, the center of gravity is low and confident. Although opposers are pummeling the top by criticizing behavior, performance, style, or process, the low center of gravity provides the quiet, peaceful, confidence of a sure-footed leader who responds, not reacts; who embraces the circumstances instead of defending; who leads through it instead of withdrawing or abusing.

## GREATEST THREAT TO LEADERS: PERFORMANCE-BASED IDENTITY

By now you begin to realize how vitally important the dimension of character, nature, identity, personhood, and being are to an effective leader. While most resources for managers and leaders focus on the top of the iceberg and skill development, it quickly becomes evident that formation in the bottom of the iceberg is an essential dimension that cannot be overlooked.

Overlooking the bottom creates a great threat to the leader. Remember the image of the well-formed iceberg? The center of gravity is well situated below the waterline, deep in the character and nature of a person. There, it provides stability and buoyancy to the whole iceberg and allows the top to rise to heights of impact in the visible arena. It is hard to tip that iceberg over.

But imagine if we could ignore the laws of physics and change the shape of the iceberg. I know it is impossible, but to press the metaphor a bit, let's imagine we could do so. What if we made the iceberg a perfect square, with half above the waterline and the other half beneath? In that case the center of gravity would be right at the waterline—which makes it much less stable than the well-formed berg. A smaller wind and smaller waves could easily make that iceberg start to roll over in the water.

Consider further that we could really defy the laws of physics and invert the iceberg with only 10 percent beneath the water and 90 percent above. Truly a strange and impossible thing to do in real life, but the image serves us well. In that case the center of gravity would be well above the waterline—high in the upper part, which we have defined as performance, skill, competence. In this scenario, with a high center of gravity, it would not take much at all to cause that iceberg to capsize. A very slight breeze and really small waves would cause that iceberg to fall. Minor criticisms and innuendos become personal challenges to this leader.

This is a condition I call "Performance-based Identity." The center of gravity is found in personal competence and in the performance of activities of leadership. It, more than anything else, is the greatest threat to every manager or leader. In this condition, we begin to define *who* we are by *what* we do. Our performance becomes our identity. Our job defines us. What we do is indistinguishable from who we are. We have truly lost ourselves in our performance.

The problem is that when a leader falls prey to this condition and performance becomes extremely good, they begin to think more highly of themselves than they should. The rules become something that others should follow, but they are above the rules and can take liberties that frequently become inappropriate. Soon they come face-to-face with reality. Perhaps it is a catastrophic moment, a whistleblower, or a sudden discovery, and the truth comes crashing down—no one is above the rules. Liberties that fuel their ego result in arrogance, which becomes exposed. With no personal character to speak of, that leader has allowed their value to become synonymous with their competence. Competence without character will always lead to arrogance.

On the other hand, in performance-based-identity, if performance begins to decline—a person receives poor performance evaluations, results suffer, and their output is hurt—they conclude they are of no value because they are defined by their performance. They think of themselves as a bad person, worthless, and their self-esteem, confidence, and self-respect plummet. Often this leads to sideline activity and behaviors in other areas to bolster self-worth. Frequently those sideline activities are inappropriate and destructive, which further erodes the sense of self-worth. Because they are so accustomed to defining themselves based upon performance, when this person's leadership is not effective, they seek performance elsewhere to shore themselves up in a false success that further undermines their moral compass and character.

This is why I say that performance-based identity is the greatest threat to leaders. It is a trap, a pitfall, a burden, a debilitating condition that dehumanizes and eviscerates the essence of a person's very humanity. Above all else, please be alert.

Years ago, when I began a new role as a leader of a regional group of organizations, I encountered one of the most painful and difficult times of my career. Sadly, the culture was highly divided and extremely focused on achieving success through numeric growth. A highly competitive environment characterized the team of about 150 primary leaders of about 60 subsidiary organizations. Numbers, size, and growth rate became the factor that determined value and worth among the leaders in the entire region. Personal identity was tied to performance.

Sadly, this long-standing priority on performance resulted in me as a new overseer having to relieve one of those key leaders every six months for major failure in moral or ethical matters that manifested in inappropriate behavior. The cost was enormous—disruptions in communities, broken marriages, wounded children, and distraction from the central mission of all of them. Significant recourses of the regional structures were spent attempting to mitigate the trend. As a relatively new leader, I wracked my brain trying to figure out what was going on. Even attempts to address the symptoms had no effect.

It wasn't until I began to call these leaders to a deeper level of Leadership Formation in the bottom of the iceberg—character, nature, calling, identity—that the trend slowed and eventually stopped. When my priority as the senior leader focused on understanding my leaders as holistic in their personhood, calling them to "who they are" as the priority rather than how successful they could be in performance, then the deeply painful failures in their lives abated. And, not surprisingly, the entire region began to see not just greater health among the key leaders but greater expansion, which became a hallmark of the whole group.

## SHRINKING THROUGH NEGLECT

Performance-based identity does not happen in a moment. It isn't a willful choice. We don't suddenly decide we want to pursue it. In fact, our very human nature seeks to avoid it since we were created to be whole. But in the face of external pressures to perform and higher and higher levels of results and outcomes that attract attention, we easily neglect the bottom of our iceberg in favor of the more noticeable activities of the top. Over time that neglect yields this horrible condition that cripples the leader. Every system of employee evaluation is built upon visible performance. It's really all we have to assess employees. In the process, we create a systemic culture in the company that prejudices our people to focus on the top of the iceberg and neglect the bottom.

When we neglect the bottom of our iceberg by being overly focused on developing skills and styles and performance, pretty soon our personal formation begins to suffer. The bottom of the iceberg begins to melt—not fast, but gradually it shrinks, little by little. Over time that shrinkage begins to show up in our behavior. Remember? We always behave out of who we are—the top is a reflection of the bottom.

As the bottom of the iceberg shrinks and our heavy focus on performance increases, the top begins to grow. Gradually the center of gravity of our very lives begins to drift upward as the bottom gets smaller and the top gets bigger. Soon, usually through circumstances, we realize we are now defining ourselves by our competence and performance. Often others close to us see it before we do. The very condition that besets us blinds us to its encroachment. We are unable to really see what is happening to us.

Sadly, many times we only see it when it is too late. We get fired, we are demoted, we find ourselves misusing money, gambling out of control, adultery, addiction—you name it. Hopefully there are good people around us at work, community, church, and family, that care enough to help.

While this is not the condition for which we were created, there is *always* a way back. But it begins in the willful choice of that same person to become open and vulnerable to accepting help to nurture the formation of their person—character, nature, and being. There are many who are willing and able to help. Family, friends, coworkers, counselors, and even God. There is hope.

# Chapter 7

# The Link to Motivation

ONCE WE ADD THE Z-axis to our understanding of people, leadership, and management, suddenly a new source of motivation begins to emerge.

The agency of leadership resides in a person, not a function. People are much more than a vessel or instrument through which leadership is channeled. People are leaders, and leadership flows inherently from people. Leadership is not merely something a person does. Yes, there are many good tools to help channel, focus, refine, and hone that leadership in its application for results. But fundamentally it is a person who has an influence on others.

People are whole and integrated, so to reduce leadership merely to functions that are competently wielded by a person undermines the very thing we seek to grow. Because a person is the agent of leadership and because people are integrated, we must consider leadership to be more than the development of skills. We have to factor in the formation of the person in order to discover the fullest impact. Leadership Formation is the careful integration of skill development and personal formation. It brings all three of the axes we have discussed into integration that builds both ability and foundation. In the integration of all three, there is synergy, and out of that synergy comes immeasurable impact.

43

The foundation of a person in the Z-axis may be the most important element of a leader's life. Just as a tall, complex building requires a strong, well-formed foundation to provide integrity and usefulness, so also a well-formed person below the waterline is the most effective foundation for flourishing. And the motivation for that effectiveness shifts with the Z-axis.

Whenever a person applies their leadership to their job or those around them, motivation flows from some source. Although not discussed much, with careful thought and reflection it is possible to trace the motivation or driving force for every person's leadership activity. It is the "why" question. People do what they do for many reasons. There are many motivations that fuel leaders within corporate roles. Each is influenced by the culture of the company and the person themselves. Most HR departments and leadership development models have identified those and then attempt to use them to grow capacity and effectiveness in their organizations.

Here are the most common motivators that drive leaders in the performance of their function.

*Demand*—Perhaps the most obvious motivator is the fact that there is a demand that must be met. That demand may be an altruistic need. Or it may be a demand of opportunity. In either case, demand is both important to the purpose of the organization, and it is a powerful motivator for people. Employees see either the payoff in meeting the need, or they experience the good feeling of meeting needs. Few people or organizations make plans without a careful analysis of demand.

*Fear*—Perhaps one of the most often used, and abused, motivators for human behavior is fear. It has been effectively leveraged in grand-scale political movements and in small departmental environments. It is even prevalent in individual relationships, where leadership is strained and needs to be asserted. It is quite effective where leadership and dominance are sought as well. Fear can motivate people to do many things. Often it is even used in religious circles to bring about a decision or behavior that is prescribed, or to gain power or influence.

*Expectation*—You don't have to go far to find people who aspire to higher levels of position and influence because someone expects it of them. Certainly, the expectations of others are not all bad. They can actually become a good point of accountability. But as an inherent motivator for a leader's trajectory and growth, expectations from others or even ourselves can become vacuous and cause disillusionment. And it can easily backfire when suddenly a person realizes they are not cut out for this, or that what they do was never their deepest desire. Expectations can come from myriad sources. Perhaps parents, self, spouse, supervisors, the role you play in a family or community, or even personal faith.

*Paycheck*—Although many people think more pay motivates more, at a certain level of leadership, money ceases to be the principal motivator for performance. With higher levels of responsibility, motivation shifts from pay to things like work environment, culture, freedom to create, time to research. Whether it is actually money or one of these alternate forms of motivation, there is a powerful incentive that comes from what a person will get in return if they perform. This contractual, quid pro quo relationship for leaders is perhaps the most visible currency in enticing heightened performance and in rewarding desired performance.

*Recognition*—Not everyone needs a lot of money. Some want recognition—in title, profile, acknowledgement, or some other means. While recognition is a function of respecting the person and dignifying people who perform well, clearly it can also have a dark side, wherein leaders presume more influence than is healthy simply due to their recognition. Further, the need for recognition that grows out of proportion can signal a deeper lack of self-esteem and confidence.

These are a few of the things that motivate people. So, it is entirely understandable why in any environment that seeks greater and greater success through performance, these would be leveraged and utilized to maximum effect to get people to perform. Companies will spend a lot to refine the use of these motivators in order to yield better performance from their employees and a corresponding increase in corporate results.

Everything about the usual methods we use to assess, hire, evaluate, and develop managers and leaders proceeds from these kinds of motivators. Both the X and the Y axes leverage one or more of these sources of motivation so that greater outcomes will result, the organization will grow, the leaders will be successful, and everybody benefits—at least in their external circumstances.

## LESSONS FROM HIGHER EDUCATION

In the last half of the 20th century, higher education began to discover some important facts about students. Although colleges and universities were created to be places of learning, the effectiveness of that learning waned, and leadership studies began to reveal that the usual formula for motivation was more than simply external incentives. In the 20th century, studies like the Hawthorne studies we've already discussed focused on worker productivity and the importance of the well-being of people over product. Those studies revolutionized the understanding of workplace dynamics, organizational behavior, and the importance of the person at work.

As a result, institutions of higher learning began to explore alternative motivators for students. Going beyond the incentive of grades, expectations, and jobs, they began to see that all people are motivated by increasingly higher levels of formation and development. The important work of Abraham Maslow was foundational to the student development movement. His pyramid of human needs begins at the bottom with survival and culminates at the apex in self-actualization. His conclusion that people are truly complex and are holistic beings requiring an intrinsic motivation opened the doors to explore how to develop humans to their ultimate goal of self-actualization.

Many subsequent thinkers, researchers, and authors—including this one—have gone on to consider factors beyond Maslow's concept of self-actualization as even more essential to the unfolding process of human flourishing. This line of thinking that goes beyond self-actualization is rooted in the growing evidence of people as created beings with an unlimited dimension that reflects our Creator. Although Maslow would include factors that comprise human character in self-actualization, the premise on which it is built is somewhat limited since we, in ourselves, are limited beings. Furthermore, it can perpetuate a more self-focused purpose that may eventually lead to a form of egoism.

However, across the United States and throughout the world, schools began to respond to this new way of thinking about human development that was more holistic. The rise of the community college movement was largely fueled by this innovation in developing people. Today colleges and universities all have entire departments devoted to student development or student success.

Recognizing that people are motivated from within by a need to flourish has revolutionized higher education. Likewise, the very rise of human resources within organizational environments demonstrates that same pattern. While these discoveries and responses are commendable, in most cases they don't go far enough. Attempting merely to meet a need for compensation, or fulfilling a demand, or recognition, or even self-development still falls somewhat short. Furthermore, the methods utilized to nurture those features to "develop the people" are principally focused upon performance and output on the X- and the Y-axis of measure. As the thinking goes, *if* a person feels valued and has their needs met, they will perform at higher levels to the benefit of the organization.

## Z CHANGES EVERYTHING

It is at this point that introducing the Z-axis to the construct changes everything. The most obvious result is that when we introduce a third dimension into an otherwise two-dimensional system, the potential combinations and interplay multiply. This heightened texture of seeing people is much more consistent with how humans were created to begin with. So, it puts us in much better position to influence and form people in a manner consistent with their nature.

Perhaps the most important change is the introduction of a new and more essential motivation—personhood and flourishing, especially when this personhood is tied to the unlimited source in how we are created. The human spirit possesses an innate urge to flourish, to blossom, to become all it was intended to become. Once we introduce the deepest element of personhood into the mix, new doors of possibility open to us. Tapping into that innate desire to flourish creates a powerful variable in helping people become everything they were created for, thereby allowing a fulfillment that is deeply personal and profoundly formational.

The X-axis measures competence in the performance of functions and provides a good measure of potential output. With some well-placed incentives and good training, that performance can be developed to higher levels of skill. The result is greater performance and a good feeling by the individual leader that they are contributing and being taken care of. The company feels good because they are getting good output for their investment.

The Y-axis provides invaluable input to determine the capacity and potential of a person to grow and contribute even more in the future. With a well-crafted plan for development and appropriate training and education, someone might even become a top-tier leader. The science of leadership development has become highly proficient and predictive. Therefore, effectively utilizing that science can inform the HR department about how to guide a high-capacity person to a rising trajectory of high performance—and everyone is pleased.

In both dimensions of the X and Y axes, the central feature is output; the external success is performance; the benefit is measurable production by a person. But let's remember that people are holistic and integrated. And people have an intrinsic urge and desire to become whole. In that wholeness, they desire to flourish. Their production may be an indicator of that formation, but it is not the sum total of it. The greatest source of fulfillment is the formation in their nature in the bottom of the iceberg where, with a low center of gravity, they find confidence, deep peace, meaning, and balance in holistic ways. Then, as we know from the iceberg, that deep formation of their identity will overflow into activities and performance that reflect the inner condition of a well-formed person.

The Z-axis introduces that internal dimension of person-hood—which isn't so much developed as it is formed. That formation isn't achieved so much by activities or tasks as it is a continuous journey of rhythms, patterns, habits, condition, and flourishing. It is certainly not easy to measure, and even less easy to prescribe. The Z-axis deals less with objectifiable metrics and more with principles that are formed deeply and then overflow in myriad ways contextually. So, in formation we cannot so much impose tasks as invite into participation with principles that shape and mold the person-hood of a leader. Sure, there are some habits that help with this, but fundamentally the Z-axis is "principle-based" much more than "performance-based." The key instrument for assessment is discernment, as well as observing the tell-tale signs of those principles in the behavior of a person that may or may not be tied to output.

Leadership Formation is the intricate interplay among the three axes of performance, potential, and personhood. The texture of that interplay is complex but effective. Integrating these three together begins to truly tap into the fullness of human potential that reflects the hope of being all that we were meant to be—with the effect of incredibly impactful influence for growth and output.

# Chapter 8

# Synergy of the Whole

ONE OF THE UNIQUE features of human nature is that we were created with a need and ability to flourish in wholeness. That is a characteristic imprinted upon humanity from the beginning. That kind of wholeness is not simply the addition of pieces until the picture is complete. It is the multiplication of factors in a process that results in more than the sum of its parts. That's synergy. And we possess the impulse not only to reproduce ourselves physically, but in every aspect—social, spiritual, personal, emotional, and in influence. That's multiplication. These are two words that capture a small part of the unique human nature we all possess.

We often describe the influence that parents or family have on us, how we become like them; we continue their characteristics and patterns. That's a result of the multiplicative feature. They are multiplied in us and we reflect them. Beyond family, we also affect and are affected by others around us. We multiply ourselves through influence, just like we are influenced and are the result of the multiplication of others in us.

Further, the synergy that we all know exists in humanity is both measurable and intangible. That intangible element is usually attributable to integration among the various dimensions of who we are—within the bottom of the iceberg and between the bottom and top of the iceberg.

When we limit our focus and attention to just two axes, X and Y, it's like we are working a typical two-dimensional puzzle. It may be a challenge to find the pieces and fit them carefully together. But really, it's just adding the pieces to each other until they all fit. We wind up with a two-dimensional picture.

But when we add a third dimension, it ceases to be a two-dimensional puzzle and becomes three—height, width, and depth. Permutations multiply and the possibilities increase. When we further add the unfathomable, infinite, and God-given texture, nuance, and intangible nature of the Z-axis to X and Y, we have great possibilities as each one forms the others. Not only is there a new axis, but the very nature of that new Z-axis is different. That not only adds the increased number of potential combinations, but the intangible nature of Z allows limitless variables and the effect is synergy. This is more than mere interaction—it becomes integration.

## INTEGRATION OR INTERACTION OR INTERFACING

Often the words *integration*, *interaction*, and *interfacing* are confused and usually conflated to mean the same thing—or at least something defined rather ambiguously. But in reality, these are three very different words with deeply different meanings that have enormous impact on understanding a leader.

Interface occurs when two or more things are placed in proximity with each other. There may be recognition, but little activity transpires between them. Each remains largely independent of the other and autonomous. There's no particular outcome, and possibly even no added value to be gained. Just acknowledgement and usefulness as separate entities with no real connection.

Interaction occurs when two or more things or people are placed in proximity with each other, and they actually work with each other. There is communication, activity, and sometimes cooperation. But the focus of that interaction is for the benefit of one or more of the participating entities' agendas. Usually interaction happens when there is benefit that occurs to both in a win/win relationship. Or at times, when circumstances are right, the interaction is to the benefit of only one of the partners. When the project or result is fulfilled, the interaction ceases. Value is added because of the benefit each receives from the other. It is like a contract, and when the objective is completed, interaction stops and both parties return to their own pursuits.

Integration is different. Integration is when two or more entities or people are not only in proximity, and not only interact, but actually influence each other at a fundamental and essential level. The very nature of each person or thing is altered fundamentally because of the involvement of the others. Not just influence but actual involvement. This involvement is much more than additive. It is multiplicative and results in synergy.

While this is more difficult to define, and hard to measure, it is more consistent with the multifaceted nature of human beings. It recognizes the multi-dimensionality of how a person is created and allows for the synergy of a fully integrated person to flourish in becoming all they were intended to be.


## BLUEBERRY YOGURT

Let me illustrate the idea of integration with an example. My wife likes to make Greek yogurt. It is pure bright-white in color. It has a clear flavor that's a little tart and sharp. It's not uncommon for us to enjoy that white, tart Greek yogurt for breakfast. In addition to preparing a bowl of yogurt, sometimes we also put a bowl of blueberries on the table. The two bowls are in close proximity to each other. I take a bite of yogurt followed by a spoonful of blueberries to make the otherwise relatively boring flavor (my opinion only) of the Greek yogurt a bit more interesting. The result tastes quite nice. I'm making a connection between the yogurt and blueberries by creating an *interface* between the two, having yogurt and blueberries in sequential bites. Each is separate and autonomous, and they act separately.

Sometimes I take a more radical step to develop the flavor more. I scoop two or three spoons full of blueberries and put them into the same bowl as the yogurt. I stir them around a bit so that the berries are largely covered by yogurt. I can see the occasional blueberry on the surface of the yogurt, and the lumps created by the berries are evident. When I take a bite, I get some yogurt with a blueberry or two in it, but occasionally I still only get the white yogurt. By eating them together, the result is an even nicer taste because they are acting together at the same time and the flavors complement one another. You see, I now have yogurt with blueberries in it, and there is *interaction* between them.

But then I take the back of my spoon and begin to mash the blueberries against the side of the bowl. Something quite different begins to happen. By crushing the blueberries and mixing the juice and yogurt, I begin to notice that the color of the yogurt changes. The yogurt begins to smooth out and there are no large, blue lumps in it. The blueberries are losing their shape. They are surrendering their juice to the yogurt. Pretty soon, the yogurt is no longer even white but a bluish color. It doesn't have lumps anymore, but it's smooth, albeit with telltale signs of blueberry pieces. When I take a bite, it's something different—more. It's no longer blueberries *and* yogurt; it's not just blueberries *with* yogurt; now I have blueberry-yogurt, something new and different. Each of the otherwise independent parts has become essentially changed by the influence of the other. This new yogurt is formed by the *integration* of each ingredient with the other.

## OPEN TO INFLUENCE

This integration requires an openness to be influenced by another. In other words, even if we have multiple entities, they must be willing and able to receive influence from the others. If they don't, it's just interfacing. Because the X-, Y-, and Z-axis are dimensions observed and applied by a supervisor or HR representative, they must be ready and able to see the effects of one on the other. They must have eyes for integration.

Over years of experience and research, we have a clear understanding of competence in just about every profession. And we also know what characteristics will likely predict capacity for future growth and influence. But now when we add a third dimension with the Z-axis, the supervisor and HR specialist have to become aware of how character might be visible and influential in each of the others. More important, how character will be the key element to the formation of the person.

Because Z is less empirical and objectifiable, new lenses must be used to see the integrative nature of character and its impact on the whole. While not entirely measurable, character is observable—mostly in the results it has in the top of the iceberg since we always behave out of who we are.

For the person who is assessing and developing people, discernment and intuition that is formed by their own personhood are the key elements to be nurtured and trusted. Observing the influence of character on competence and its contribution to future capacity cannot be entirely taught by skill development. And it is not completely empirical or objectifiable. Certainly, skills of observation, and the ability to look for the tell-tale signs of character in shaping performance, are important. But, the most important element of using the Z-axis in assessment will be "soft." In other words, this ability will need to come from the very nature and character of the one who is assessing and developing it in the other. Like recognizes like.

If the HR specialist or supervisor assessing leaders is not attuned to their own sense of identity, character, and nature, it will be difficult for them to observe, much less assess it in another. They will certainly be able to achieve some level but only to the extent their own skills have been developed to see the character of another. Lack of discernment and intuition will limit that ability greatly.

The holistic, integrated nature of every person derives from the remnant of the One who created us, which continues to have an image in us. It includes dimensions that are in both the top *and* bottom of the iceberg. We are physical, emotional, social, intellectual, and spiritual beings. Externally measuring only competence and capacity severely limits the full synergistic potential of every person. We tend to want to reduce things to measurable, repeatable steps that can be trained. We shy away from things that are "soft," less measurable, and that require discernment. Because of that propensity to objectify as much as possible, we easily fall prey to neglecting the bottom of the iceberg, where character resides and which is so formative in all of the visible expression of life in every person. However, embracing that dimension and opening ourselves to its influence provides a new pathway to employee and leader assessment and development.

Perhaps the guiding question in the synergy of integrating the three axes of competence, capacity, and character is simply:

> When the pressures of performance and achievement assault you amid the myriad forces of expectation, where do you center down to be renewed and to rediscover who you really are?

We have been programmed and trained to "do" as a means to solve problems and answer questions. Every organizational system has been built with activity in mind. So, in responding to that question, the temptation is great to simply develop a new task, or checklist, or just try harder. Seeking renewal and flourishing in that vicious cycle of performance only feeds the need for more and ends up in the unfulfilling hollowness of performance-based identity. Finding the center of gravity in the unseen bottom of the iceberg is the only source of confidence, stability, and motivation.

It's from this deeply formed place of character in the bottom of the iceberg that moral fiber, ethical balance, disposition, attitude, and motivation flow. Maturing and growing in this dimension involves the formation of patterns of living and thinking. It is wrought from rhythms of learning and growing and fueled by the vulnerability of formation and integration in our own lives. When channeled through the competence of skill and performance, this intrinsic personhood of an employee and leader can flower in vibrant fulfillment of becoming all they were intended to be.

Chapter 9

# Effects of Leadership Formation

## SO WHAT?

COMPETENCE WITHOUT CHARACTER YIELDS arrogance; character without competence results in irrelevancy. No matter how much good character a person has, if it is not translated into real effect, there's no point. It does no one any good. Leadership must have some effect in order to be useful. And there must be something that results in the influence of a leader to qualify them to assume responsible positions in moving an organization forward to fulfill its mission. So, there is an empirical element to leadership that is observable and measurable. Even though we have been focusing on the more intangible Z-axis, this observable effect should be the natural overflow of a leader's growth. Measurable results are vitally important and provide relevancy to the very presence of a leader.

One of the most compelling questions that drives organizations and corporations is "what difference does it make?" Or, "how does this help to achieve our goals?" Organizational theory and leadership models have all explored the ancillary factors that contribute to effectiveness, and these questions are ultimately the ones that command attention, time, and money. Most budgets are not built with the purpose of funding things that do not further the purpose of the organization or increase the bottom line. Even altruistic, charitable non-profits are closely monitored to ensure fiduciary efficiency in order to maximize impact. Therefore, "so what?" is a legitimate question for leaders to ask.

How does the Z-axis contribute to the mission, goals, and outcomes of the company? Does adding an emphasis on the Z-axis really help an organization fulfill its purpose? Does it add value to the already proven and commonly used 9-box of competence and capacity?

The great "so what" is a significant part of the development of a leader and is equally central to Z-axis Leadership. A leader (a person) is not just developed or trained but *formed* in the confluence of the three axes of X, Y, and Z. This Leadership Formation, while good and noble, is truly only helpful when it finds effect in the influence the leader actually has in creating a corporate culture and trajectory for a business, school, church, or organization to fulfill its goal.

So, what is the effect of Leadership Formation? Why is the integration of the Z-axis together with X and Y so vitally important? How can we expect that synergy to be expressed in visible situations?

The effect of the Z-axis is not simply in its inclusion in the employment processes of recruitment, development, promotion, and assessment of leaders. It is really found in the interplay and integration with all three—X, Y, and Z. When mixing all of the factors involved in Leadership Formation, synergy results. When character, competency, and capacity begin to integrate one with the other, a dynamic develops that offers new and long-term effects. And the result is a pathway and future that is not simply built upon outcomes and quarterly performance but also on health, perseverance, adaptability, responsiveness, and moral fiber.

## DESCRIPTIVE MORE THAN PRESCRIPTIVE

Rather than *prescribing* expectations, let me *describe* what generally happens as a result of the influence of a leader who is actively living out the "bottom of the iceberg." That person's identity is constantly being formed as they integrate competence, capacity, and character. Remember, we always behave out of who we are, so the formative nature of a Z-axis leader will look different because they are being formed differently with the full integration of the three axes together.

We won't hold up prescriptive expectations for performance since that will only invite the very performance-based focus we seek to moderate. That would simply encourage an external source of motivation demanding compliance rather than nurture a holistic and principle-based effort to form leaders. By describing the principles and descriptors, we are able to recognize the effect and then nurture them.

1. Holistic—This descriptor has already been introduced in basic form. It is the fundamental presupposition that guides how we view people. When a manager looks at an employee, or any other person for that matter, what do they see? It is quite easy to look at someone as a means to an end, whether that is for relational gain, political influence, or to fulfill a task. But limiting a person to merely what they can do reduces the value and essence of that person as the principle agent of influence. Recall that people are created with an innate nature that is holistic.

   When a person is encouraged to embrace that view of themselves within the context of their daily work, it taps into the core fiber of their nature. They are more deeply formed, and the resulting confidence, focus, and moral foundation becomes the strength on which all of their activity is built. In fact, their leadership activity is shaped and motivated by that very self-image. They begin to see their coworkers, clients, and even supervisors as whole persons, each with competence and capacity in specific areas, but more fundamentally as people with a story and their own vocation and purpose.

2. Integrated—Every person is multifaceted. To expect performance in behavior without a deeply rooted passion and an understanding that makes sense is to bifurcate a person and ignore the totality of who they are. Compartmentalized people are more likely to overstep the lines of propriety than those that are held in check by the various dimensions of their souls. Here is where ethics and moral fiber are shaped so that when one part of an employee is tempted to cut corners, the other part holds them in check. Passion may drive behavior to excess, but reason mitigates the extreme. Peer relationships may pull an employee to the edge of propriety, but deep security in identity holds steadfast against the flow. Rationalizing may conclude that skimming for personal gain is justified, but deep realization of being created with an image that has dignity and worth counteracts the contortions of the mind.

Because of the multi-dimensional creation of our nature, we have an intrinsic "checks and balances" system that was put there to guide us and hold us fast to a centered identity.

3. Diverse Application—Because the identity is sound and well-formed, it is not easily shaken. "Who I am" is not in question by a well-integrated leader who is formed around the three axes. In that confidence of self, a leader is able to truly consider the most effective way to use their influence in any context. Knowing that in some situations they may be challenged or even confront difficulty, the Z-axis leader can proceed with leadership activities that they know will be best for the company. Their identity is secure, their moral compass is clear, their nature is quietly confident, and they need not be shaken. They seek to please only an audience of one.

When leaders are liberated from the oppression of defining themselves by what they do, they find immense freedom in acting in a manner consistent with their identity to further the goals of the company. That comes from a well-formed person that has deep integrity.

4. Permeability—As one of the necessary characteristics of integration, permeability is also dependent upon a strong sense of personal identity. The leader who is confident in their identity in the bottom of the iceberg is not afraid to accept input, gather diverse perspectives, consider and reconsider issues, and allow others to shape their thinking and actions. Being permeable to people around them, these leaders not only gain the best input for making their choices, but they empower others around them by valuing their input and accepting their influence. This is not a threat to authority. Because authority flows from a source much more important and deeper than position or title, leaders like this do not need to appeal to their position and can even show their openness to others in mutuality.

5. Humility—Much like permeability, this descriptor requires a deep sense of identity that is not based upon performance, position, or politics. Humility is an honest recognition that none of us knows everything. In reality, none of us knows as much as we think. Accepting that reality allows a leader to hold a posture of humility in which they are willing to receive input from others and at times be corrected by others. We all know people who seem to be the "know-it-all." No one likes that, and few are willing to work with, much less follow, that person. Allowing others to inform, shape, and influence us demands an attitude of humility.

   Don't mistake humility for weakness. In fact, weakness is the blustery, overly confident person who often is compensating for profound insecurity. There is no stronger attribute than a humble spirit.

6. Integrity—Often misconstrued as a moral code, integrity is really nothing more than the integration of various parts to create a whole that is more than the sum. When all the individual pieces of a bridge are put together, they create a complete structure that does more than any of the pieces could separately. They fit perfectly, and they depend upon

each other. When the weight of traffic passes over the bridge, it is the integrity of the pieces constructed together that hold the weight and fulfill the purpose.

In similar fashion, personal integrity is when all of the dimensions of a leader are integrated with one another, like the blueberries and yogurt, and the result is that they depend upon each other, are formed by each other, and together the result is a purposeful, meaningful, whole life that flourishes. The moral aspect of integrity is drawn from the bottom of the iceberg, where identity is forged through recognizing that the values, purpose, and image are a reflection of the Creator and finding expression through daily activities of performance.

The best example of this kind of integrity is found in the biblical personality of Jesus of Nazareth. He was clear in his claim that he was a full reflection of his father, God. And that shaped his nature, values, and priorities such that even in the face of criticism, persecution, and ultimately death, he remained committed to fulfilling his purpose.

7. Formative—Most people assume that process is a means to an end, that we go through steps that will ultimately yield a completed result. When we add the Z-axis to our view of leadership, it becomes quite clear that there really is no terminus, but there is a trajectory toward which we walk, trying to help employees move to greater and greater effectiveness. In reality, the very journey of Leadership Formation is formative. It is the journey itself that is the formation. We don't tell employees to "do the seminar on Z-axis leadership so you will have that skill." We develop systems and resources that place people on this path that will continue and will yield ongoing formative steps that improve both outcomes and fulfillment in people. Because formation is situated within circumstances, every experience can be formative, especially the tough ones. When a character flaw shows up in a poor choice, it is a moment to both correct the behavior but more importantly, to form the underlying foundation through character formation. That is not easy in systems and cultures that are usually

punitive and seek recompense. HR departments that only seek to protect the company from litigation, loss, or reputation will often miss the formative opportunity. Because they seek only the top of the iceberg results, the deeper opportunity at forming the character of a person is lost, and often, rather than being the agent of integrative leadership, they perpetuate the assumption that people are simply the tool to fulfill the purpose of the organization. Including the Z-axis will always introduce the formative possibilities for redemptive and developmental work in Leadership Formation.

8. Moral Compass—To a significant degree, conversations about what is moral have disappeared from employee conversations and organizational leadership structures. Perhaps it is because clearly defining what is moral and what is not is a rather difficult task. Most people feel it is necessary to use great precision and measurable terms and formulas in order to remove, as much as possible, all subjectivity from employee assessment. The result is that principles of leadership and evaluation shift to ideas and concepts that are both tangible and empirical. Because morality is much less visible, empirical, and objective, it defies that kind of limitation. Therefore, people and organizations may shy away from it as being unattainable.

Perhaps another reason conversations about morality have been laid aside is a growing opinion that everyone has their own. Or further, that because the world is growing more and more diverse, each culture defines morality differently; therefore, in order to be inclusive and accept the diversity, we must not impose on others. "You do you . . . What's wrong for you is okay for me." Morality becomes a highly relative concept that elevates the individuality of each person, and the greatest virtue is tolerance or acceptance.

Whatever the reason, the question of having a moral compass in leaders and employees is often overlooked as a significant part of how people are formed intrinsically. This loss is to the detriment of both personal identity and corporate identity, especially when circumstances become difficult. In this absence, it is quite easy for companies, organizations, and even churches to assume that what is moral is what is expedient. Of course, the difficulty is that when done in this way, even our moral compass becomes subject to external performance and results. If it works, it must be okay—a form of utilitarianism. So once again, the performance and results of a person become the standard for shaping their moral compass.

In reality, our moral compass is formed deep within our identity. Morality is forged in the inner identity of recognizing that we all are created and have a common image that is fundamentally innate to us all. Our humanity is common among us. That starting point has been ingrained deep within every person. The inner nudges and nuances of rightness and wrongness, of good and bad, of evil and righteousness, all proceed from that deep place that is unseen. The tinge of conscience or the weight of guilt, the joy of sacrifice and the power of empowerment, all find their source in that deeply forged foundation of identity. Allowing that intrinsic morality to find expression in behavior begins to anchor our performance in a way that breaks the bonds of enslavement to judging ourselves based only upon outcomes and results. This is central to the nature of the Z-axis. Encouraging employees to be attentive to that formative process of a strong moral compass helps them find meaning and fulfillment, both personally and professionally.

Z-axis leaders may not talk about their moral compass out of deference to others, but the anchor that informs their living and secures their path is a manifestation of that deeply nurtured morality. Having honest conversations about the need to pay attention to our individual and corporate moral sensitivities helps us to develop in the areas of propriety and civility. Furthermore, the more this inner identity is formed, the greater the ability to operate in a highly diverse environment where collaboration goes beyond tolerance to acceptance. It is on this basis that organizational culture and leadership maturity is formed. Though unseen, a well-formed moral compass in a leader will have profound influence in that person's disposition, attitude, confidence, and decision-making.

9. Ethical—In the wake of historic and high-profile business catastrophes that are traceable to unethical behavior, most companies and even nations are seeking to strengthen the ethical framework that guides their systems. Often companies seek graduates from universities that emphasize character formation in their educational systems. Many national governments have created departments of "anti-corruption." Businesses form codes of ethics and ethics review committees. Educational institutions have ethical review boards for research and practice. Culture increasingly prefers the competent employee who evidences a strong moral fiber and high ethical standards to the hot-shot performer.

I have had many people ask if ethics are absolute or relative. My answer is "both." Ethics is nothing more than actions that actively reflect an inner moral fiber. "Morals that find expression in behavior" is how we define ethics. Without the element of practice and application there are no ethics. So, the real question is, "How do our practices reflect the moral compass on which we build our lives and our organizations?" For companies and even societies, the consensual work of the people comes to a shared understanding about ethics that is evidence of a common "sense" within the people regarding what is or is not ethical. This common sense is traceable to the shared nature we all possess. That commonality among us is attributable, in this author's opinion, to the nature of the Creator from whom we all proceed.

While ethics may be applied differently, depending on the circumstances, the principles that guide those practices are rooted in an absolute morality that is shaped by recognizing our common human nature. For those with a faith in God, that human nature is imprinted and shaped by God who created humanity. So, ethics are absolute in their source but may be manifested relatively in the context and through the lens where they are lived.

In every case, Z-axis leaders will be guided by ethical behavior that is tied directly to the moral compass which shapes those practices and patterns of living. Helping people to think about ethical practices and tying those to the inner nature of their moral compass is an exercise in forming people in the bottom of the iceberg. The benefits are not simply to the company in providing healthy and ethical employees, but it is also beneficial to the people themselves in discovering their value, meaning, and fulfillment.

# Chapter 10

# Getting from Here to There

## POSSIBLE STARTING POINTS

SO, WHAT'S A PERSON to do? While all of this might be revolutionary in how you approach your role as a "people manager" or as someone charged with shaping the HR systems of a company, how can you start the process of living these principles in practice? Here are some ideas:

1. *Think deeply*: By this, I mean to say, that introducing the Z-axis into the process of hiring, evaluating, guiding, and developing leaders cannot begin with specific tasks that may be empirically measurable. It has to begin with deep reflection, understanding, and consideration of the principles in your own thinking. Don't move quickly to action steps. Begin with thinking deeply. If you are the type that requires disciplined schedule, then set aside thirty to forty-five minutes daily for two weeks to consider the principles of character, identity, and formation in your own life and others. Consider supplementing that with articles and podcasts that nurture this priority. The Z-axis in particular, and Leadership Formation as a principle, is a mindset, a disposition, even an entire approach to life. It involves seeing beyond the visible and measurable

to the intangible—even spiritual—elements of the essence of a person. It cannot simply turn into just another tactic or skill to be acquired. The principles of Leadership Formation must permeate the rhythms of your mind such that your outlook about yourself and others is transformed.

Once you understand the idea and the nearly limitless dimensions of introducing a third axis of consideration into leadership, allow that understanding to marinate so that your approach to leadership becomes fundamentally altered, with new texture and depth. Clearly this will affect your actions, but it does not start with changing actions. To go back to the iceberg analogy, as the bottom of your own iceberg becomes formed afresh in understanding the dimension of personhood and character, you will find that the natural outflow of your activity in the top of the iceberg will begin to be different.

2. *Accept the importance of personhood as vital to leadership*: Likely this doesn't even need to be stated. But just to be clear, who we are is more important to leadership than what we do. What we do is the natural outflow of who we are. External sources—regulators, stakeholders, consumers, members—may place a heavy expectation on you for performance and results. That creates a tendency in you as a leader to fulfill those performance-based expectations, even at the expense of higher priority items like Leadership Formation, ethical behavior, a moral compass, perseverance, and identity. Those same external sources will only be interested in matters of personhood and character when they impinge upon the results of performance. You, and those key leaders with you, are the ones with the burden of keeping the bottom of the iceberg well formed, with a low center of gravity. Allow your deep thinking to take you past the intellectual idea of Leadership Formation to the internal conviction that it is vital to healthy, effective leadership.

3. *Seek new sources of understanding people*: Most leaders who manage people and oversee systems of human resources have

a tried and true arsenal of tools to help them. Those are very important. However, in most cases they are built on the presumption that the dimensions that need the focus are two: performance and potential. Or, in other words, competence and capacity. Begin to look for new sources that open the horizon and nurture your newfound understanding of what the nature of people really is—in the hidden dimensions of character, nature, identity, and being. This is where you will begin to find the deepest motivations and features to empower people to their fullest. These sources may be as simple as others around you, or more existential tools about the nature and formation of people. It may be through your church. It may be as simple as merely opening up conversations with people or conducting surveys to discover the deepest needs your people have. Perhaps you eschewed the required college courses on philosophy or theology. But often those are the places where we get a good view of the questions that the Z-axis deals with.

4. *Begin small*: When a new idea captures our imagination, for some reason we think we have to move immediately to implement big plans to change the world. Check that impulse. Allow the new ideas to soak and saturate your thinking and begin with small steps that bring others with you in your expanding outlook. Perhaps discussions with staff members, or reading new sources together. That may lead to identifying some key points of adjustment in the system and procedures that allow for the Z-axis to emerge as a vital part of working with people.

In the process of hiring, evaluating, guiding and developing people, begin to introduce new language that treats the questions of their own sense of personhood, how they see themselves, and what motivates them. Clearly there are limits to the line of questioning around inner and personal matters. But approaching your role with ears that are tuned to hearing about their moral compass, intrinsic values, self-identity will begin to alter the entire atmosphere of the organization.

One small step that may have huge ramifications may be to adjust assessment reviews to include more qualitative dimensions that require discernment of the supervisor on the Z-axis. Once you have internalized the principles of a three-dimensional pattern, you will find that you also have eyes to know it when you see it. Your own discernment will be heightened. Looking behind a person's adaptability, resilience, ethical challenges, spiritual nature, and moral confidence will yield new insights. You will begin to notice the synergy of those things integrated with behavior in the performance of their duties.

5. *Adjust assessment tools:* Sadly, most assessment systems are designed to measure output. Few exist to assess character—and for good reason. The intangible nature of who we are is much more elusive to quantify. That's why any initiative on the Z-axis will require the use of qualitative systems that attempt to discover and discern the formation of a person.

Adding new tools explicitly to uncover some of these dimensions may be a good pathway. Or perhaps adjusting the ones you already have by expanding their scope would be better. Adding key questions to evaluative surveys you already use, or encouraging supervisors to be sensitive to issues of character and personhood opens the door to discovery. It won't all happen at once. Like any new horizon, it is discovered and it unfolds step at a time, never all at once.

6. *Learn as you go:* The very process of implementing a new mindset or a new dimension of human development will have within it unfolding lessons you can only capture as you go. Because you are creating a culture and an employee base that is unique to your context, allow the principles to introduce new lessons. Embracing the lessons along the way will allow you to grow, refine, deepen, and focus this new priority on character as a key element to effectiveness. Often, the process is the best teacher. We learn and refine as we go forward.

7. *Build a network:* Identify and bring into regular relational connection like-minded people who help to nurture your

thinking in this integrative, three-dimensional way. It doesn't have to be people you work with. In fact, some of the best who can help you are beyond your workplace. Some even in other fields of work. Perhaps external consultants attuned to this priority, like the team at Kingdom One. Often someone with a more spiritual outlook can help you tap into the deeper and nuanced nature of the iceberg. That might be a counselor-coach, a pastor or priest, or a retired leader with a strong sense of identity. Allow these people to reflect with you specifically on the subject of integrating performance, potential, and personhood in your own thoughts and in the specific challenges you face.

8. *Introduce the iceberg to the organization*: You don't even need to make the connections with the X- and Y-axis initially. Build into your staff training sessions or onboarding a treatment of the iceberg. That becomes the first step to explaining the whole three-dimensional approach to assessment. In my own leadership history, when I began to teach, discuss, and introduce the nature of personhood as represented in the iceberg analogy by itself, I saw an almost immediate adjustment of behavior that mitigated undesirable traits in leaders. Later, I was able to make the connections with the X and Y axes.

   Merely bringing the iceberg image to the attention of people allows that intangible human factor in them to resonate. I am convinced that when you take thirty minutes to introduce the topic of personhood and explain the iceberg to them, you will have an immediate connection from them. You will see a positive response and requests for more understanding. I have seen this happen all around the world in senior executives of top businesses, higher education leaders, medical professionals, and church leaders alike. But before you introduce this, be sure you have taken the time to reflect and internalize the themes the iceberg is intended to convey.

9. *Offer methods to keep the bottom of the iceberg well-formed*: Because every organizational context is different, there are no

"cookie-cutter" methods to help people focus on and deepen the formation of who they are. But I can offer categories. From these three categories you may be able to design specific practices that are appropriate to your situation:

a. Habits—Encourage your people to develop repeated behaviors, which will inevitably turn into habits. And habits have a way of shaping the deeper dimensions of identity and personhood. Clearly these habits should be of a nature that focus on the inner dimensions of a person's life and nourish their character. It is much like creating a diet that will affect our bodies after a long period of eating. If we eat a steady diet of food that is unhealthy, we will become unhealthy. Likewise, when we regulate or intentionally create a diet of habits, they will have an effect on our life. Perhaps it's a habit of:

- Daily reflection in the morning or at night;
- Regular meditation;
- Periods of solitude and silence;
- A time of devotions daily;
- Going without a meal weekly to think instead.

Habits can also include certain behaviors that eventually shape the nature of the inner person. Like:

- Always saying "thank you";
- Beginning every conversation with asking the other how they are;
- Telling the truth, no matter what;
- Acknowledging the other in the conversation by using their name;
- Always looking at a person's eyes when speaking to them.

These are simple things. But habits have a powerful long-term impact on shaping the bottom of our iceberg.

When that effect is fulfilled, it then begins to characterize who we are as people, and that begins to fuel itself to new depths.

I often illustrate habits as a type of exoskeleton. That's when a life form has the skeleton or shell on the outside of the body. That external shell puts pressure on the body to mold it into conformity with the shape of the shell. Habits do that. They are external behaviors intended to shape the interior of our life.

Eventually, when the habits, or disciplines, of life have had their effect and the bottom of our iceberg has been influenced by them, the result is that out of that newly shaped inner life, actions and behaviors will be affected so that what we do is consistent with who we are. In that cycle of formation, then, the skeleton of identity begins to shift from the exoskeleton (outside framework) to an endoskeleton (inside framework). By whatever name you give them—habits, disciplines, repeated behaviors—you can help your people develop a pattern and rhythm that highlights and forms the inner being of personhood and character.

b. Accountability—Often in organizational leadership, when we talk about accountability we speak of behavioral accountability in which outsiders hold us accountable to do what we say we will. Politicians are the most obvious example. When they promise to deliver, the public holds them accountable to actually do what they say they will do. If they don't, then they are voted out of office and replaced, with the hopes that the next person will. In education, accreditors hold schools accountable to standards of education and may remove that if they are not good enough. Financial institutions are tightly regulated by state and federal agencies that hold them accountable to the proper management of money that does not belong to them.

Part of the role of managers is to hold employees accountable to fulfill what they agreed to do in their yearly work plan. If they don't, there are consequences—sometimes no pay increase, or perhaps demotion, or even termination.

But accountability has a much more important and formative place in Leadership Formation. Beyond behavioral accountability, there is *identity accountability.* This still requires others around us. Identity accountability is when people hold us accountable to behave in a manner consistent with who we are. In other words, that the top of our iceberg is consistent with the bottom. That's really another word for *integrity.* When two or more things fit and work together to fulfill the purpose for which they were created, they have integrity. Remember the bridge I mentioned before, for example? It has integrity when all the pieces fit together and successfully sustain the weight of the cars that drive on it. A building has integrity when all the pieces fit and connect properly so that it stands firm and sustains the test of time and weather.

Likewise, people have integrity when who they are is consistent with what they do—the top of the iceberg is consistent with the bottom. Creating systems, structures, or possibilities for people to be in a relationship of accountability allows for a few close to them to be able to see their behavior, discern their character and provide accountability that holds them secure. Such programs are like the guy-wires for the tall radio towers. They connect the tower from various angles and hold it upright against the wind. Having people nearby in a relationship of identity accountability provides that kind of support to holding a person straight and strong in ethical, moral, and character balance amidst all the forces that vie for their attention and lure them into possible shortcuts in performance.

These may take the form of small work groups, job-alike groups, or life coaches. The possibilities are many. Be creative to structure systems that provide accountability for more than just the performance but also are sensitive to the nature of formation in people.

c. Reflection—This is much more difficult to catch, as it is very intangible, highly relational, and even spiritual or metaphysical. It involves encouraging people to develop patterns of solitude specifically to reflect on themselves, their values, their life, and those they love. For people with faith, this involves God and often is described as communion.

Although this is much more intimate and personal, creative ways can be devised to encourage reflection—even if it is not able to be monitored. At the very least it signals that the organization sees the inner life of its people as being just as important as the performance and potential they represent. There are many possibilities. Perhaps it includes resources like:

- A "thought for the day";

- A "quiet room" that allows people to take five minutes to disconnect and ponder the press of work demands;

- Urging employees to take their days off or vacation;

- Resource seminars that speak to wellness and work-life balance.

The risk of every organization—business, school, corporation, church, or club—is that what it does can become so important to the people in it that their very lives devolve into becoming merely cogs in the wheel of success. That results in short-sighted shallowness. Beginning with the very basic paradigm of how we hire, evaluate, guide, and develop people, these same organizations are able to create profoundly rich environments where people not only perform but where they flourish. And in their flourishing, everything they accomplish becomes an overflow of meaningful contribution to both the purpose of the organization, as well as the very purpose of their vocation.

# Chapter 11

# A Quick Summary

## PANORAMA OF POSSIBILITIES

THE MODERN DISCOURSE ON leadership has saturated the marketplace with styles, techniques, and theories, offering polished strategies for application but often neglecting the deeper, formative elements. We've grown comfortable seeing leadership as a science of functional behaviors—an external shell that can be trained and applied. But this reductionism misses the organic, holistic identity of the leader—the essence of who they are. The true vibrancy of leadership lies beneath the surface, in the foundational "bottom of the iceberg."

Modern talent systems like the 9-box HR grid reinforce this truncated view. With an X-axis for performance and a Y-axis for potential, leaders are evaluated on their capacity to produce and to grow. While practical and measurable, this two-dimensional paradigm reduces employees to commodities—evaluated only by what they can do and what they might do for the organization. When that happens, both the supervisors and the employees begin to see themselves as compartmentalized beings: professional vs. personal, public vs. private. And they develop an outlook that is transactional, leaving meaning and value to be determined by outcomes.

The result is a crisis—not of competence or capacity—but of essence. We have good people doing good work but missing a key dimension: the internal, character-driven core of the leader. There is a third axis—a Z-axis—that introduces character, personhood, and identity as equal partners in assessing and developing leaders.

## LEADERSHIP IS MORE THAN FUNCTION

Ask ten people what leadership is, and you'll likely get ten answers. But nearly everyone can recognize leadership when they see it. That intuitive quality is not the sum of skills or the repetition of good behavior. It is something deeper: influence.

Leadership is fundamentally the ability to influence others. That influence is varied—seen in business, politics, community, faith—but its effect transcends style and technique. It emanates from within the person. While techniques matter, they are merely vehicles. The core is the leader's inner person—their integrity, moral compass, sense of purpose, and grounding.

Reducing leadership to technique alone is like describing salt only in terms of flavor. There is something about the nature of the leader—their being—that gives form and weight to their doing. Therefore, real leadership must involve more than training. It must involve formation—the shaping of the inner life of the leader.

## CRISIS OR LIMITATION

We're not in a leadership shortage because we lack smart or passionate people. We're in crisis because our focus is skewed. We train for skill, not for soul. We want leaders who can execute tasks but forget to nurture the identity from which those tasks spring.

Formation is not development. Training enhances what a person can do. Formation shapes who a person becomes. Skill can be practiced, repeated, and measured. Character is formed through rhythms, values, reflection, accountability, and community.

When leaders are not well-formed in the bottom of the iceberg, we begin to see performance-based identity: where a person believes their worth is equal to their results. This distortion either leads to arrogance when they succeed or despair when they fail. And it is one of the greatest threats to effective, enduring leadership.

## X-AXIS—COMPETENCE IN PERFORMANCE

The X-axis reflects a person's ability to perform. It is grounded in Theory X leadership models, developed many decades ago, where people are assumed to require external motivation to produce. Performance is measurable and tied directly to results. For years, this has been the main lens through which employees are assessed.

Systems like forced distribution or "grading on the curve" create environments where performance becomes the singular metric. This mindset can drive short-term gains but erodes morale, innovation, and collaboration. Performance alone cannot define value. While it is necessary, it is not sufficient.

Leaders shaped by only the X-axis see their teams as functional assets. And they themselves are reduced to tools of productivity. In such systems, training becomes merely behavioral modification. High performance becomes the currency of advancement, and character becomes a footnote—if acknowledged at all.

## Y-AXIS—CAPACITY FOR POTENTIAL

While performance gauges what someone is currently doing, the Y-axis considers what they *could* do. This dimension of capacity is less visible but crucial for succession planning and leadership pipelines.

Potential is assessed through patterns of growth, adaptability, self-awareness, and motivation. Leaders with high potential are often placed in development programs or farm systems, similar to the minor leagues in baseball. These systems prepare high-potential individuals for future leadership by rotating them through roles, mentoring them, and challenging them in new ways.

Development plans are key tools in stretching the potential. They connect current performance (X) with future possibility (Y), offering personalized pathways for growth. But even the most carefully crafted plans can fall short if they neglect the formative dimension—the Z-axis—of the individual.

## Z-AXIS—MAKING IT WHOLE

This third axis, the missing link, completes the Leadership Formation picture. The Z-axis introduces character, nature, identity—the "bottom of the iceberg." It is about who the leader *is* rather than what they do or what they could do.

Drawing from Maslow's hierarchy of needs, we understand that people are motivated by more than salary or recognition. At the apex is self-actualization, but even this falls short unless we recognize the full dimensions of the imprint of our Creator. When that is integrated into leadership, we open the possibility of limitless formation.

The Z-axis deals not in competencies but in wholeness. It speaks to motivation, humility, resilience, and integrity. In crisis, a leader formed in the Z-axis doesn't crumble. Their identity is not defined by circumstances. Their center of gravity is low—anchored deep beneath the surface. As a result, they respond with clarity, not reaction; with peace, not panic.

## LEADERSHIP FORMATION: INTEGRATING THE X, Y, AND Z AXES

True Leadership Formation is the convergence of all three axes: the competence of performance (X), the capacity for influence and potential (Y), and the character of personhood (Z). It is not enough to build skills or to track growth trajectories. The leader must be formed in their whole being.

Imagine a 3D grid: The X and Y axes give us a flat grid—a surface upon which we can plot performance and potential. But the Z-axis gives depth. It moves us from a chart to a structure. And it reminds us that leadership does not rise solely through effort but is stabilized through formation.

In this three-dimensional paradigm, we don't simply ask, "What can this person do?" or "What might they be capable of?" We also ask, "Who is this person becoming?" That question reframes our systems, our assessments, and our developmental strategies. It forces HR departments, executives, educators, and mentors to consider the leader not just as a worker but as a whole person.

A development plan in this model does not merely outline skills to be learned. It also invites the leader into rhythms of reflection, accountability, coaching, and personal formation. The workplace becomes more than a training ground. It becomes fertile soil for holistic flourishing.

## THE LINK TO MOTIVATION

When we see people as integrated beings, the sources of motivation also change. Leaders are not moved only by fear, expectations, or even a paycheck. At their best, they are moved by a sense of calling, meaning, and desire to live from a coherent identity that overflows in their performance.

Introducing the Z-axis opens the door to that deeper motivation. People are created to flourish. They want to become. And when their influence flows from this inner wholeness, the results are more than productive—they are transformative.

X-axis leadership is driven by what can be seen and measured. Y-axis leadership is inspired by future potential. Z-axis leadership is shaped by who the leader is in their essence—and that makes all the difference.

## CONCLUSION: THE WAY FORWARD

Leadership in our time doesn't lack resources. It lacks wholeness. The missing link is not another technique, model, or framework. It is character. It is the deep well of personhood that shapes every expression of leadership.

To form leaders, we integrate the three axes. We train skills (X), develop capacity (Y), and form the person (Z). In this integrated synergy of *Leadership Formation*, we raise leaders who are resilient, trustworthy, impactful, and flourishing. The iceberg holds the metaphor: the deeper the bottom, the higher the potential. Let us form leaders from the inside out—leaders with a low center of gravity, grounded in character, anchored in calling, and equipped to lead with enduring influence.